Praise for *Water*

"*Water Witchcraft* is a fluid mixture of a [...] practices flowing from the fertile watery realms of Annwn and Avalon. The author has listed many interesting items from tradition, often combined with thoughtful and creative concepts of her own. I enjoyed her accounts of her direct magical experiences with water and the practical advice that she offers based on those experiences. This is a very thorough beginners' book that should prove useful and inspiring to those seeking a path of water magic."

—R. J. Stewart, author of *The Underworld Initiation,*
The Way of Merlin, and other books

"Come away with Annwyn Avalon and immerse yourself in the wonderful, magical world of water witchcraft. Water witch Annwyn Avalon will deftly guide you through the flowing deep wilderness of all aspects of water magic, regaling you with magical tales and folklore rooted in Celtic and Brythonic lore. In her book *Water Witchcraft,* Avalon meanders through the history, magic, and deep mythology of water with vast knowledge and experience. No pebble is left unturned in this enchanting book, as you are swept up in a magical voyage of spells, meditations, incantations, and useful tools for the modern witch."

—Patricia Weston, author of *White Witch Patricia Weston's*
Book of Spells & Magic

"Water, one of the primal elements of nature, has long deserved a book such as Annwyn Avalon has brought into the world with *Water Witchcraft.* Featuring rituals of connection, charms of healing, and goddesses to reach out to, this book isn't just a primer, it has something for witches working with every drop, from sacred well to local spring. The magic within feels as though you've been practicing it your whole life from the moment you pick up this book."

—Amy Blackthorn, author of *Blackthorn's Botanical Magic* and
creator of Blackthorn Hoodoo Blends

"Annwyn Avalon takes us on a fascinating journey that explores the various types of water and their associated folklore, deities, and magical beings. In addition to explaining how to work with different forms of water, her unique practices and exercises serve as a guide for becoming a water witch and using the enormous power of this element."

—Sandra Kynes, author of *Sea Magic: Connecting with the Ocean's Energy*

"A gorgeous guide through the world of water myth and magick. Annwyn Avalon lifts the lily pad on the watery nature of our own spirits and shows us how to embrace our own mermaid, selkie, and well spirit. If you have ever gazed at the ocean and longed to touch its heart, this book offers a path to do just that."

—Courtney Weber, author of *Brigid: History, Mystery, and Magick of the Celtic Goddess* and *The Morrigan: Celtic Goddess of Magick and Might*

"Annwyn Avalon's enchanted book dares to peer deep into the waters—the mirror betwixt the worlds—revealing unto the reader a rich trove of spirits, ancient deities, eldritch beings, stories, and lore. Deeply practical too; *Water Witchcraft* reveals also tools, substances, rites, charms, and spells, both traditional and innovative, enabling the reader to fully explore, connect with, and employ water in all its forms as a potent vehicle for power and transformation."

—Gemma Gary, author of *Wisht Waters—Aqueous Magica and the Cult of Holy Wells, Traditional Witchcraft: A Cornish Book of Ways*, and other books of magic and witchcraft

"Annwyn Avalon shares her deep water wisdom in this insightful book that is empowered with well-researched lore, traditional folk practices, and sound magical principles. *Water Witchcraft* is a truly comprehensive work that reflects not only an intimate understanding of the nature of water in its various forms, but also details the myriad ways in which water can be used to effect positive change in our lives. Annwyn deftly channels various streams of folkloric knowledge into a practical approach that is reflective of the wisdom of the past, while being eminently accessible to the modern-day practitioner of water magic."

—Jhenah Telyndru, MA in Celtic studies, priestess, author, and founder of the Sisterhood of Avalon

Water Witchcraft

Magic and Lore from the
Celtic Tradition

ANNWYN AVALON

Foreword by Skye Alexander

WEISER BOOKS

This edition first published in 2019 by Weiser Books, an imprint of
Red Wheel/Weiser, LLC
With offices at:
65 Parker Street, Suite 7
Newburyport, MA 01950
www.redwheelweiser.com

ISBN: 978-1-57863-646-4
Library of Congress Cataloging-in-Publication Data available upon request.

Cover art by Shaheen Miro
Interior by Deborah Dutton
Typeset in Weiss

Printed in the United States of America
IBI

10 9 8 7 6 5 4 3 2 1

Dedicated to the Gwragedd Annwn, Melusine, Sulis, and the water spirits that guided my mind and heart and forced my fingers to write when I was lost in the whirlpool of my mind.

Special thanks to the Green Flame and Fire Storm that gave me such a strong foundation for my magical craft, holding oceans of possibilities. To the Circle of the Rising Moon who honored my voice and gave rise to my water craft. To Duston and Tiffany who loved, encouraged, and believed in me.

Contents

Foreword   ix

Introduction   1

Chapter 1: The Magic of Water   9

Chapter 2: River Witches   35

Chapter 3: Sacred Well Witches   67

Chapter 4: Lake Witches   107

Chapter 5: Marsh Witches   133

Chapter 6: Sea Witches   153

Chapter 7: Local Water Spirits   191

Chapter 8: Mermaids and Finfolk   207

Chapter 9: Water Witchery   237

Conclusion   263

Bibliography   266

Internet Resources   269

Index of Magical Exercises   270

Foreword

Maybe we sense a sacred connection with water because our bodies and our planet are composed largely of water. Maybe it's because, as science says, we emerged from aquatic sources. Long before the theory of evolution developed, however, creation stories from around the globe told us life on earth originated in the world's waters. According to Babylonian mythology, for instance, the water goddess Tiamat was the mother of everything, including the other gods and goddesses. The Aboriginal Australian story of the Rainbow Serpent also credits a water deity with bringing us all into existence.

Water goddesses, such as Anuket, Sulis, Oshun, and Danu (for whom the Danube River is named), figure prominently in the folklore of cultures everywhere. Our ancestors believed ponds, rivers, and seas teamed with spirits of all kinds. In his book *The Secret Teachings of All Ages*, Manly P. Hall wrote "According to the philosophers of antiquity, every fountain had its nymph; every ocean wave its oceanid. The water spirits were known under such names as oreades, nereides, limoniades, naiades, water sprites, sea maids, mermaids, and potamides." Usually we link water with the feminine or yin force, which is why so many water entities are described as female.

Today we continue to revere the earth's waterways—the Ganges River, Lake Manasarovar in Tibet, Glastonbury's Chalice Well, the grotto at Lourdes, Crater Lake in Oregon. At these places of power and mystery, modern-day pilgrims seek healing, purification, consecration, and transformation, just as they did centuries ago. Even people who don't recognize the spiritual nature of water intuitively understand its curative properties. Who hasn't felt invigorated when sitting near a waterfall or cleansed after a dip in a cool lake? We go to spas to "take the waters" and flock to the seaside to rejuvenate our minds and bodies. Those who live near the ocean, as I did for thirty-one years, quickly become aligned physically, emotionally, and psychically with its shifting tides.

Countless legends also tell us about the magickal nature of water. According to Celtic lore, evil spirits couldn't cross running water. Faeries resided in wells. Lakes served as portals into other realms. The River Styx in Greek myth led to the Underworld. In the Arthurian legends, the Lady of the Lake gave Arthur power by gifting him with the sword Excalibur. And we've all tossed coins into a pool or fountain hoping our wishes would come true.

Water plays an important role in many magickal traditions and practices. It's one of the four elements that serve as the building blocks of life (along with fire, earth, and air). In the tarot, water is represented by the suit of cups. Three of the twelve zodiac signs—Cancer, Scorpio, and Pisces—are water signs. In spellwork, a witch's magick chalice and cauldron are considered water tools. A still pond serves as the perfect scrying device—reputedly, the noted 16th-century seer Nostradamus sat for hours gazing into a bowl of water to divine the future.

When we think of water magick, we often think of cleansing tools and crystals, taking ritual baths, and formulating potions or elixirs. In *Water Witchcraft*, Annwyn Avalon offers a wealth of information about these practices; however, she also shares ways to use water magickally that you may never have considered before, such as freezing it to bind an enemy, making poppets of snow, and melting ice to release stuck energy. She also explains how to tap the properties of dew, fog, mist, hail, rain, and sleet—even the steam from your morning shower. Each type of water has its own unique qualities and applications in witchcraft. For example, water collected during a thunderstorm is imbued with dynamic energy that can fuel aggressive spells. Water from a peaceful lake can ease stress and promote harmony.

The entities who guard and occupy earth's waterways also possess a wide range of characteristics and powers. Some are benevolent, others mischievous or downright dangerous. Annwyn (whose name refers to the Otherworld in Welsh mythology) describes these mysterious beings, such as the seductive Lake Ladies and the dark magick of marsh witches, and explains how to deal with them, should you encounter them in the physical or spirit realm.

Water Witchcraft is also a cornucopia of sea-based legends and lore from Ireland and the British Isles, and includes magick spells that draw upon aquatic ingredients. Early mariners believed fervently in water charms and employed them widely; however, modern-day witches can use gifts from the sea in their spell work, too. Annwyn shares her abundant knowledge of natural water tools: shells, sea glass, smooth river stones and stones with holes formed naturally by running water, sea salt, fossils, and quartz crystals that contain water bubbles (known as enhydro). Water plants—lotus flowers, seaweed, algae, and kelp—possess magickal properties as well.

In this treasure trove of water witchery, you'll find exercises, blessings, charms, incantations, spells, and rituals. I especially liked her spell to bind companies that harm our oceans. She recommends placing "their logo inside a clam or oyster shell. Wrap the shell with bindweed, tangled seaweed, or a fisherman's net. On the waning moon, take it to a place where three rivers meet and bury it near where they intersect, calling upon the local spirits to aid you. You can also take the shell to a crossroads, preferably by a graveyard, and leave it in the center. In either case, walk away and don't look back."

Annwyn encourages you to "develop a personal relationship with water." Visit watery places—lakes, streams, oceans, marshes—and experience the special energies that exist there. Communicate with the genius loci or spirit guardians of these places. Learn about the plants and creatures that live there.

At this crucial time, when we're experiencing massive pollution of the world's waters, and when human-induced climate change threatens our seacoasts, marine life, and future generations, Annwyn's call to honor the spirits of the waters rings loud and true. Immersing yourself in this intriguing and informative book will give you a greater appreciation for the life-giving water from which we originated and on which we depend for our continued existence. Water Witchery will also help you attune yourself to the archetypal feminine force operating on our planet and in the universe. And it will empower you to work with this wondrous creative energy to generate healing, abundance, and happiness for yourself and others.

Blessed be,

Skye Alexander, author of *Mermaids: The Myths, Legends, & Lore* and *The Modern Guide to Witchcraft*

Introduction

Water flows through our bodies and across the earth; we depend on it for life. Our bodies consist of 70 to 80 percent water and we need it to survive. Three days without water and we cannot live. Our bodies feel rundown when we are dehydrated. And it's not only our flesh and bones that require water—our souls seek it as well. Many of us are inexplicably drawn to the ocean. Body and soul, we long to be in the water.

As far back as we can remember, humans have been intimately connected with water, both physically and spiritually. We associate it with deities, spirits, souls, and creatures of other realms who find their homes in or near bodies of water that are often the setting for supernatural occurences. We work with water in a sacred manner for our lives, for our children's lives, and for the lives of the deities and spirits we find there. Throughout history, hundreds, perhaps thousands, of named water deities and spirits—and just as many obscure and unnamed ones— have appeared in myth and legend, and folklore is full of tales of magic wells, talking wells, water nymphs, great sea gods, and more.

Witches have long been associated with these water spirits and their supernatural powers—take, for instance, folk practitioners who dowsed for water using a forked branch. But there are many other types of water magic and water witchcraft. Being a water person myself, I set out to explore water magic as a craft, and discovered a host of magical practices based around the sea, wells, springs, rivers, and other bodies of water. My goal in this book is to share with you some of what I found. I hope to provide you with the history, folklore, and mythology of water, as well as some spells and tools that can help modern witches and magical practitioners pursue a water-based practice. Although these traditions and practices appear worldwide, this book will focus mainly on those rooted in Celtic and Brythonic lore. I hope the information given here will enrich your life and your overall magical praxis, and encourage you to work through both the mundane and astral realms to heal, protect, and nourish our precious water sources.

In this book, we will explore the folklore and mythology of the Celts and those that influenced them. We will discover how they worshipped the water, the ways in which they honored it, and the relationships they had with the spirits and supernatural forces dwelling within it. Since this is a witchcraft book, we will examine and consider these stories from the perspective of those who see truth in the supernatural. Whether you view them as accurate accounts passed down through the ages, as folktales exaggerated to provide insight into unknown phenomenon or cultural values, or even as moral lessons is up to you. Regardless of how you approach them, these stories provide access to the Otherworld and clues about how to interact with it. As such, they can act as the foundation for a modern practice for all watery-natured witches.

Water Witchcraft

A modern water witch is simply one who works witchcraft with water and who is deeply connected to water and the spirits that dwell within it. By water, I do not mean just the ocean or large lakes, but also rain, snow, marshes, rivers, streams, and ponds, as well as many other forms of natural water that call to us.

Water witchcraft is very similar to sea magic and sea witchcraft. In fact, water witches often blend sea magic with their craft, focusing on tides and moon cycles, gathering their tools from the shoreline, and integrating shells, driftwood, and sea plants into their workings. But sea witches typically stick to the seashore, whereas water witches can be found just about anywhere—near lakes and rivers, around holy wells, beside streams and ponds. And although there is no universal "water magic tradition," most sea witches and water witches tend to work in a similar manner, their practices only varying based on their chosen body of water, their training, and their path preference. What binds them together is water in its many forms.

Simply put, water magic is a craft based around bodies of water that uses water plants and other natural objects found near the water, and works primarily with spirits and deities that are associated with water. This craft is rooted in ancient water lore that developed in the traditions of country folk and was preserved in both ancient Pagan and Christian practices that centered around the British Isles, Brittany, and other Celtic regions. While not every topic presented here is drawn from the Celtic tradition, this information is gathered from lands where the ancient Celts exerted a strong influence and where their descendants preserved their traditions.

The Celts believed that water was sacred; it represented a liminal place, a portal to the Otherworld, Annwn, Avalon, and the ancestral realms. When the Romans occupied Britain, their culture mingled with and strongly influenced many of the Celtic practices. In many cases, the Romans simply took over ancient sacred sites, just as the Christians later did. This helped to preserve these practices, albeit slightly modified to fit into a Roman or Christian frame. In many cases, when Christianity began to take root in Britain, the new faith mingled with Celtic Pagan traditions, again preserving remnants of the water cult that had existed there from time immemorial, simply changing the names of many local rivers, springs, and sacred wells to the names of saints. This happened again in the many cases of faery women who later came to be known as witches. It is important to note, however, that the numerous stories of these faery women, many of whom were water fae, often depicted them as holy and benevolent beings. In fact, in some stories, they are even likened to God and the Holy Virgin. This was not always the case, however, with many of the finfolk.

When the Christians arrived and found that almost every body of water in Britain and other parts of Europe was named after a female water spirit, they simply renamed the sites. This is why there are so many wells named for Saint Mary or Saint Anne, or many other female saints whose names were co-opted to promote the new religion but still honor the *genius loci*, the protective spirit of the place. A good example of this is found in Sequana, goddess of the Seine, whose shrine sat at the head of the river that runs through Paris. The local spring that feeds the river was later renamed after a male saint, Saint Sequanus. But despite these attempts to erase the Celtic water cult from history, much of it is preserved in the folktales, stories, and lore passed on from generation to generation, in some cases through the lineage of faery women, whom many later figures can claim as ancestors.

Magic in the Molecules

Japanese entrepreneur, photographer, and author Dr. Masaru Emoto (1943–2014) wrote several books on the structure of water molecules and how they are changed and affected by location, the human mind, and negative and positive energy. To demonstrate that vibrations and various types of energy could affect it, he subjected water to different types of music and recorded how the structure of the water molecules changed when exposed to classical music and then to rock and roll. He also compared the crystalline structure of water from many different locations, comparing and contrasting water from places like holy wells and sacred sites with water from places that were polluted by pesticides and other substances and considered unsanitary.

Using a very powerful microscope in a very cold room, along with high-speed photography, Emoto photographed newly formed crystals of frozen water samples drawn from different locations and subjected to different sound waves, music, and words. He found that the crystals of water drawn from one area were often vastly different from the crystals of water drawn from another. He also found that classical music produced beautiful crystals, while heavy rock and metal music produced crystals with scrambled circular patterns. Water taken from polluted areas would either not crystallize at all, or crystallize into distorted, misshapen forms.

Next, he began experimenting with language, using words like "love," "hate," "thank you," and "you fool" and photographing the results. He found significant differences in the water crystals produced. This led him to form the hypothesis that molecules of water are affected by our thoughts, words, and feelings. He also studied the effects of prayer, ritual, and blessings, and found that they too changed the character of the water. Although his theory is controversial and has been attacked by many skeptics, Emoto has documented his work with hundreds of photographs and written several books on the subject, including *The Hidden Messages in Water*, which was a New York Times bestseller.

In my opinion, Emoto's work is ground-breaking and validates our craft. When we combine his visual evidence that vibrations, words, thoughts, and locations can vary the molecular structure of water with the reverence that ancient cultures had for water, water deities, and holy wells, we have evidence based in both history and science that water magic works. Moreover, this proof comes from someone who is not a magical practitioner. Did Emoto simply find, through scientific methods, what our ancient ancestors already knew?

We know from Emoto's work that even the slightest word can create a change in a water molecular's structure. And we know that how that word is spoken influences the outcome of that change. Later in the book, we will dive into specific modern water-magic methods that draw directly on Emoto's insights, like creating gemstone elixirs and flower essences by infusing water with the energy and vibrations of flowers, plants, or stones to enhance its magical properties. What is important to note here is that, when we put these concepts about water together with Aleister Crowley's definition of magic as causing changes to occur in conformity with the will, *we can actually see the energetic and vibrational changes that we call "magic" in the changing of the water crystals.* This is very important to understand. In fact, it is the theory on which this entire book is based.

Chapter 1

The Magic of Water

Two of the most famous magicians in the world—Aleister Crowley and Dion Fortune—have described magic as change in accordance with will. In water magic, we exert our will and intent through our physical and energetic bodies to perform rituals and spells that can change the properties of water. This is why water magic can be so powerful. Moreover, if we accept that words and intent influence the structure of water molecules, and we define magic as change according to will, and we consider will and intent to be virtually synonymous, we can state a clear and simple formula for water magic:

Intent + water + delivery method = magical change

In a way, we can even see the magic take place!

When we look at water magic as a practice, working with either small quantities (rain, ponds, or wells) or large quantities (rivers, lakes, or oceans), this formula makes it very clear that chanting, spells, circumambulation, incantations, sigils, and many other magical tools can be incorporated into it with incredibly powerful results. This is evident from the ancient beliefs of the Celts and Romans, right up to the modern science of Dr. Emoto. With some practice, we can work the perfect combination to influence and direct specific change.

Almost every sea or water witch I have met is a bit of a magpie who collects shells, wood, glass, and other items from the water to create shrines or altars. I find that water witches are attracted to bottles, bowls, and other vessels. We are often found beach-combing or searching the banks of rivers and lakes. Water witches are often good at water scrying and divination with shells or bones found along the shoreline. Many love to swim, boat, or surf, and we are often found covered in flower petals and salts floating in the bath.

The astrological charts of witches with a strong penchant for water witchcraft often indicate this—not only their sun signs, but also their ascendants and moons, may be in the water signs of Cancer, Scorpio, and Pisces. Many are drawn to some sort of mythological water spirits or creatures like mermaids, selkies, and Lake Ladies.

Outside, water witches work with sea water, brackish waters, lakes, rivers, swamps, snow, hail, rain, ponds, canals, seasonal creeks, sacred wells, and other places where water resides. Inside, they work with teas, sacred baths, healing waters, hydrosols, distilled waters, and water-based sprays. The following chapters go into these techniques in more detail and give examples and exercises for you to practice. Really, there is no limit to water magic!

WATER BY ANY OTHER NAME

Water exists in three states: liquid, solid, and gas. Water magic works with all three and all three, for our purposes, are considered to be water. In my practice, I use the Celtic *triskele*, or three-armed spiral, each arm of which represents one of the three states of water (see Figure 1). In this book, we will work primarily with water in its liquid state, but here are a few fun ways to work with water in its other two states:

Figure 1. The Celtic triskele, or three-armed spiral.

- Freeze water to stop an enemy, or to freeze something in place through the act of binding. Binding is the magical act of stopping or containing energy or intent. Frozen water in the form of ice or snow is often used in binding rites to prevent an action or to

The Magic of Water

keep someone from performing an action you want
to stop.

- Defrost water to get stuck energy flowing again,
  to thaw a frozen heart, or in spells involving new
  beginnings. Through sympathetic magic, the act of
  thawing brings the perfect energy to spell work that
  unbinds, gets things moving forward, or gets something started. It holds energy similar to that of the
  Chariot card in tarot. Place a taglock—an item that
  represents a person like a photo, hair, nail clippings,
  something indicating their date of birth, or even
  clothing items—for the targeted person or action
  in a bowl of snow or ice and allow it to melt while
  chanting or charging the item. Once it is melted,
  you can empty the melted snow or ice into running
  water to speed up the spell.

- Etch protection sigils or other magical symbols and
  brief incantations on frosted or frozen windows.
  Make snow poppets to use in healing and cursing;
  use freshly fallen snow to make wonderful wintry
  cleansing water.

- Draw beauty symbols or sigils of cleansing on the
  bathroom mirror using the steam from a shower.
  Use fog and mist in visualizations or in the physical
  world to access the Otherworld or to clear the mind
  of fog.

The energy of rain and storms is particularly powerful. Witches, and especially sea witches, have long been associated with storm energy and with controlling the weather. There is nothing like sitting on the banks of a large body of water watching a terrible and powerful storm roll in. Many water witches enjoy this type of weather, and we pull energy from it, sending out spells and letting the roaring winds and waters weave the magic. I collect water everywhere I go, including water from storms. I label and date the containers, including information on the type of storm, its location, and how I plan to use the water. Summer sun showers possess beautiful warm energy, and sun shower water can encourage growth, health, and creativity. On the other hand, hail and lightning storms pack a very powerful punch that can be useful in magical workings that need an extra push. Storm water can also be used to curse and is useful for protection.

All types of water were used to predict fortune, cast spells, break enchantments, and heal. Meeting a woman with a full water jug was believed to bring good fortune, while meeting one with an empty jug foretold troubles ahead. In some areas, taking an article of clothing from a witch who had cast against you, tying it to a rock, and throwing it in a lake before moonrise protected you from the witch's magic. In other areas, just throwing a cursed object into a lake at midnight was enough to break the enchantment. In Orkney, water used to wash a sick person was thrown out a door or gateway to transfer the sickness to the first person who came through it. Here are some other types of water that have magical properties, along with some of their uses:

- *Black water:* a modern invention that is sold in many stores. It is infused with trace "fulvic" minerals that turn it black and make it very alkaline. It can be used during the dark half of the year's Sabbats and for shadow meditations, shadow work, shadow magic, or anything else that is nocturnal. Some wells produce water that is black or turns items touched by it black, but this water is not safe to ingest, while black water purchased from a store is. St. Joseph's Well, located in the crypt of the Lady Chapel of Glastonbury Abbey, is widely considered to have black water. A few others are mentioned in later chapters.

- *Brackish water:* occurs where fresh-water rivers meet salt water. This mix of fresh and salt water can be substituted for fresh or salt water, and carries its own calming but darker energy. The shorelines are liminal places full of healing and death, balance and bane, with yarrow growing among the poison hemlock. Use this water in magic to merge with or to enter the "betwixt and between."

- *Dew:* collected at dawn on May 1st (Beltane), it brings power to beauty rituals and spells.

- *Fog and mist:* useful especially to access the Otherworld. Mist can be used as a portal, especially during the liminal hours of dusk and dawn. Meditating, walking, or sitting in a light trance state while a fog or mist rolls in creates an environment that calms the mind and allows you to connect with or even enter the Otherworld.

- *Hail or sleet:* collected during or after a storm, it comes from the sky in a furious frozen state. Keep it frozen or melt it and store it in a bottle. It is generally used for cursing and can make a great base for War Water, an aggressive formula containing water and rust that is used for physical and psychic protection, spiritual cleansing, and to place or reverse a curse.

- *Marsh, bog, swamp, and canal water:* dark dirty water that is imbued with decaying plant matter and has become stagnant. These waters can be used for darker magic, ancestral work, and to hide, cover, or mask. Swamp water is full of mystery and poison. Toads, snakes, and spiders lurk within the grooves of hollowed trees and mingle with the reeds peeking above the surface of these waters. Swamp waters can be found all over the world, and can be used for any type of magic.

- *Mud:* water and earth mixed together. It is mysterious and messy. You can use it as an earth element and to bury old worn-out cycles, or for grounding.

The Magic of Water

- *Sea water:* has unlimited uses. It can be used for work with spirits and water deities; with a prayer or blessing, it can be used as holy water, as it is already salty. It has many useful healing properties and can be used for healing, protection, charming, and cleansing. It is also useful in banishing rituals.

- *Fountains and pools:* Water pumped through homes, heaters, and fountains is sometimes chlorinated. When I first started to encounter water spirits, I looked to the old and traditional ways. As my practice expanded, however, I found that these waters also had both personality and spirit and could be used in my personal work. If you live near or around these types of manmade waters, you can still develop a relationship with them and use them for specific and personal purposes.

- *Pond and lake water:* typically calm and serene and often resembles a mirror. Use lake water to discover mysteries. Lakes are considered portals and many creatures dwell in and under them. These waters are good for relaxation or revitalizing spells. If you are in an argument with someone, use lake water to "calm" the situation. Because of its still surface, lake and pond water is also useful in scrying—divining or foretelling the future by gazing. Lakes are like mirrors, and so support self-reflection. They can also be used in watery mirror work and vision journeys as a portal to the watery realms.

- *Rain water:* ideal medium for water magic. I work with three major types of rain: water from sun showers, "dreary water," and water from thunderstorms. Sun-shower water can be used for healing, nourishment, and solar magic. It is a great base for Florida Water—a perfumed water made with various herbs and flowers. What I call "dreary water" occurs when a light rainfall continues for days, typically accompanied by gray skies and cool temperatures. Collected over several days, this water is great for shadow work, resting, rejuvenation, invisibility, and protection. Thunderstorm water is fierce. It can be used in aggressive magic, cursing, and in any spell that needs a really big power-packed punch! It's particularly effective if you can safely collect and work with water from a large storm like a hurricane, but always remember to make safety your priority.

- *River water:* fast-moving water that can be used in conjunction with or in place of the Chariot card in the tarot to speed things up. If you need something to move along quickly, find a river and work with its water. It is also useful for aggressively cleansing your energetic body of impurities and negativities. Sit in a river with the directional flow hitting your back to enhance a purging or cleansing visualization.

The Magic of Water

(I often use the phrase "Send it down the river!")
Launch little boats made of twigs and leaves and
send them down the river with the intent of getting
rid of something or someone. Rivers, canals, and
streams can be used for spells involving moving forward, change, getting unstuck, and sending things
away. The Celts believed that evil spirits could not
cross running water, so rivers are also useful for
escaping an astral enemy. Remember, however, that
bodies of water that flow freely will have energy
different from that of stagnant canal systems.

- *Snow or ice:* can be kept frozen or placed in a jar or
  bottle and allowed to melt. It is great for winter
  water magic. Like all ice magic, it can "freeze" your
  enemies in place. Likewise, the act of defrosting will
  help you get "unstuck" and move to a more flexible
  place. It can also be used to defrost an enemy's icy
  heart. Draw sigils in snow for temporary binding or
  to help unbind.

- *Spring and well water:* fresh waters that literally "spring"
  up from below the ground. These waters are usually
  crystal clear and are often associated with mystery,
  mythology, and folklore. They can be used in healing magic and to connect with water fae. They were
  also used to remove curses and enchantments, and
  to place curses—often for a fee.

- *Waterfalls:* some of the most beautiful waters. Some flow all year, while others are seasonal. This water is useful in cleansing and purification, and in rites of birth and beauty.

This list shows how water, as an element, can be worked with in all its various physical stages and states. But it can also be worked with as an *entity*—as a spirit or otherworldly being. An example of this can be found in the old Irish tale of the Horned Woman, which was first recorded in the late 19th century, although its origins are believed to be much older. This tale tells of a woman who is tricked into letting twelve horned witches into her home. The first witch to appear has one horn; the second has two; and the pattern continues up to the twelfth witch, who, of course, has twelve. The witches begin to put enchantments on the woman, her home, and her family.

When the woman becomes distraught by her lack of power over the enchantments in her own home, she goes to the well, which speaks to her, helpfully revealing its knowledge of magic and counter-cursing. When the horned witches direct the woman to collect water from the well using a sieve, the well tells her how to patch the sieve and then teaches her how to defeat the witches' enchantments. The story is important, because it portrays the well as an entity and makes it clear that the water (or the spirit within it) is speaking directly to the woman. Many modern water witches tell me that they speak to water or that water has spoken to them.

WATER ALTARS AND SHRINES

No matter what their chosen path, most witches pursue their magic in a sacred working space like an altar or a shrine. An altar is a sacred surface on which to create and work magic, as well as a place to commune with the spirit(s) it is dedicated to. Altars can also provide a setting for divination. Shrines are structures erected in honor of a divine spirit that serve as a focus of devotion, prayer, energy, and meditation. Shrines are gifts to the spirits they honor. They may be simple, or adorned with beautiful offerings and objects of significance. Shrines tend to be permanent; altars can be built and taken down as needed.

Creating a water altar or a water shrine is a magical act in itself, an act of devotion that establishes a sacred space in which you can honor or work with water and its spirits. A great deal of magic, energy, and intent goes into creating shrines and altars. In fact, the act is akin to a form of moving meditation and I am always very grounded after I create one. Be sure to keep your altars and shrines clean. Freshen up the offerings they hold and rearrange them periodically so that their energy does not become stagnant. There really are no rules for creating shrines and altars, but here is a general overview of how to set them up and how to use them.

Exercise: Creating a Water Altar

Begin by selecting a space that is safe and that will go untouched by tiny hands or curious guests. If at all possible, set up your altar facing west, as that is the direction traditionally believed to align with the water element. If this isn't possible, orient your altar toward the closest body of water or the one that you work with regularly, so that you consistently align yourself with it.

Once your table or other surface is set up, cleanse and consecrate the space in the spirit of water and dedicate it to any water deity or spirit with whom you currently work or wish to work. If there is no particular spirit you want to honor, or your practice tends toward the agnostic or atheistic, consider dedicating the altar to a particular body of water or perhaps just to water in general. If you are not currently working with a particular spirit, but you would like to connect with one, create the altar as directed, but leave the dedication open until your spirit's identity has been discovered or established.

Next, cleanse the altar space, both physically and spiritually. Of course, you can use any method you like. But to get you started, I have included some very basic ways to create holy water below. Choose one and work with it in this exercise.

Gather your holy water and consecrate your sacred space by sprinkling the altar with it, saying:

With my breath,
With my heart,
And with my will,
I consecrate this space.

Once the space for your altar has been cleansed and con-secrated, you can begin to set it up. You'll find a list of items you may want to add to your space later in this chapter. Once the items have all been cleansed, dedicate the altar to water, or to a water spirit or deity.

HOLY AND SACRED WATER

Using holy water to bless or cleanse objects, yourself, or others is a great alternative to smudging. Though I love to cleanse by burning dried herb bundles, such as Mug-wort, the use of smoke and fire to purify is not always safe or convenient. As water witches, we can use water in the same manner without those disadvantages.

There are numerous sources from which you can collect sacred water, like holy wells or sacred rivers or springs. This water is generally already magical, but you can add an additional charge to it with your intent or an incantation. Please note, however, that not all water from sacred sources is safe to drink. Be sure to do your research and find out if the water can be ingested.

There are also many ways to create your own sacred water. Here are just a few of them:

- *Charm water:* Take nine white quartz stones from a running river, disturbing the water as little as possible. Then retrieve water from the stream, collecting it in the same direction as the flow. Heat the quartz stones until they are red; then drop them into the water. You can bottle this water and use it in curative spells or in magic. To align with the old folk method, I recommend that it be used nine times or nine days in a row.

- *Moon water:* Here I tell you how to make Full Moon water, but you can also make New Moon, Dark Moon, and Quarter Moon water in the same way, depending on the cycle of the moon. During the Full Moon, cleanse your sacred vessel and place your selected water in it. If you have water from a sacred source or a local drinkable source, use this; if not, work with spring water. Let the vessel filled with water sit under the Full Moon. Make sure the moonlight shines on it for a good portion of the night. You can also leave the water out for three nights and add quartz to enhance it. You can cover the vessel with a lid or plastic wrap so that the water isn't contaminated with rain water or bits of nature, or you may decide that these are suitable additions and work with them as well. When you are satisfied that your water has been sufficiently charged, bring the bowl back to your altar or sacred space and whisper prayers or blessings over it. Ask your spirits, deity, or guides to bless the water; then bottle it and save it for the future.

- *Hagstone water:* Hagstones, also known as holed stones or bored stones, are stones that contain a natural hole formed by running water. They were thought to resemble the vaginal opening and birth canal, and were used in sympathetic magic during childbirth. They have been used in this manner since at least the 1500s and, most likely, long before that. Sometimes these stones are called cramp stones, presumably from their use to ease menstrual cramps and labor pains. Steep the stone in water for several hours; then use the water to wash the afflicted body part. Water made with a hagstone can be used for charm water, in healing, and as holy water.

- *Floral water:* Sacred water can be created with various flowers and plants by combining them with water in various ways (see chapter 9). Create a blend of flowers or herbs and steep them in your selected water to create an infusion. Then use the infusion in your magic.

- *Gemstone elixirs:* Combine gemstones and water to create sacred, magical elixirs. There are two different ways to make these elixirs—the direct and the indirect methods (see chapter 9). Remember that not all gemstone elixirs are safe to ingest and some stones cannot be placed in water, as they will be damaged.

- *Salt water:* Use salt to transform ordinary water into holy water by placing it in a sacred vessel and dropping three pinches of salt into it. Place your wand, athame, or other energy-directing device into the water with its point facing into the vessel. Twirl the water three times and say:

Three pinches of salt
Twirled thrice about
I hereby cast all bane out!

- You can use any of the many varieties and forms of salt to create holy water. Salt is also used on altars to represent the earth element. Himalayan pink salt is often used in healing; Dead Sea salt is prized for its curative properties; black salt is used for protection, exorcism, and shadow work; sea salt can help to align you with ocean energies. Traditional Ceremonial Wicca favors salt circles and sigils, and it is widely believed that a salt circle forms a barrier of protection. Some believe that salt repels spirits and so tend not to use it in rituals except when actively banishing spirits. In Scotland, it is often used to protect from witchcraft, while in Ireland, it is used to cure faery sickness. In Japan, people carry small bundles of salt for protection. Be sure to add a prayer or blessing when creating your salt water!

- *Silvered water:* Silvered water is created by dropping a silver coin or other silver object into water that has been obtained from a liminal place. Place your silver object into a sacred vessel and pour your selected water over it, filling up the bowl. Bless the water with a prayer or incantation—folk custom recommends that you repeat the words nine times. You can call on the spirit of a sacred well or on an ancient water maiden using words like this:

Maiden of the sacred well,
Bless this water,
Bless the well.
In your sacred spiral swell,
Bless this water,
Bless the well.

- Label your water and store it in a mason jar with a tight lid. In Scotland, silvered water was often used by faery doctors to cure the curse of the evil eye. There are also many accounts of it being used to heal and cure, and in various other forms of magic.

TOOLS FOR WATER WITCHES

A water witch uses many tools. These vary from witch to witch and practice to practice. What I give below is not a complete list; as you progress through this book and along your path, you will discover new tools—both conventional and unconventional. The ocean is a wonderful place to find tools like shells, bones, sea glass, and other strange objects that have been washed up by the tide.

The sacred vessel is perhaps the most important tool for water witches. I have several different ones that I use for different purposes—the chalice that customarily sits on my altar, as well as a cauldron. But my most sacred vessel is a beautiful blue bowl that was consecrated with the waters of Glastonbury's Chalice Well. This treasured bowl resonates with Glastonbury's energy and folklore.

Years ago, when I first wanted to start working with a sacred vessel, I was given the vision of a sacred blue bowl in a meditation, so I set out to find one. At about that same time, I learned of the Glastonbury Blue Bowl and the history that surrounds its mysterious connection to the Holy Grail. I use my sacred blue bowl to make floral waters, gemstone elixirs, and moon waters. Chalices can also be used in this manner, as can glass or crystal bowls. Black bowls are often useful for scrying.

There are many tools that water witches use in their magic besides sacred vessels and holy water, however. Shells, bones, and driftwood washed up along the shore, hagstones found along a river bank, even a magical mirror that can function like the clear reflective surface of a calm body of water can all be added to a water altar or a sacred space. And these and other objects can be blended with water to make healing elixirs and potions.

Other tools that are useful to water witches include a mortar and pestle, wands, and ritual blades. Some use ritual musical devices like bullroarers to cast a circle (but some don't cast a circle at all!). Indeed, it is almost impossible to cover all the diverse tools that water witches use. Below, I give you a list of just the most basic tools. You can purchase most of these items new or make them yourself; you can gather some of them from nature; you can even get some of them at an antique store or second-hand shop. Just remember to cleanse all second-hand items thoroughly to remove residual energies that may interfere with your magic.

- *Bathtubs:* A modern water witch's magic circle is frequently the bathtub, which can become a sacred place for spiritual cleansing.

- *Bones:* Bones of all types are often found in the "tween" places on the banks of rivers and the shores of sounds, lakes, or oceans—washed up on the sand or tucked away in the weeds. They can be powerful spirit allies, and can be used in a variety of magic and divination.

- *Bowls:* Bowls can hold anything from water for scrying to offerings, and even sacred water for water workings. My sacred bowls are the tools I use most frequently.

- *Cauldrons:* These are often used to represent the Goddess, but can also be used in place of a chalice. Be warned, however: Do not use cast-iron cauldrons for water-fae magic! This is a great way to anger the water fae, and water's nature is often to retaliate.

- *Chalices:* These can be used to represent the Goddess or the female form, as well as for holding wine for offerings and libations. Shells can also serve as chalices.

- *Combs:* Magical combs are associated with mermaids, but can also be used to comb your hair and entwine wishes, spells, and magic into braids.

- *Crab claws:* These are great tools to use in binding and reversal magic, or when something needs a little pinch. I also like to use them when I'm working rituals of solitude. They can be found washed up on the beach.

- *Jars, bottles, and vials:* These can be used to store gemstone elixirs as well as magical and enchanted waters. They can also be enchanted and turned into magical bottles that hold potions or used to gather water from a sacred source.

- *Mirrors:* These are closely associated with mermaids and magic, and also function well as portals and scrying devices.

- *Pearls:* Pearls are incredibly powerful, very beautiful, and highly prized. They come in many colors and shapes, and can be used in ways similar to crystals in magic.

- *Plants:* Virtually all witches work with herbs, flowers, and plants. Flowers growing on the bank of a river or in a sand dune are particularly effective. Roots that have washed up on shore can be incredibly powerful talismans. Charms can also be crafted from seaweed—for example, bladderwrack is a very powerful plant that is used by many witches, not just sea witches.

- *Sea glass:* These frosted bits of glass are often found on the sea shore; if you are lucky, you may find river glass as well. These are best used for color associations—to remind you of the places where you found them, or to recall what your intuition is telling you.

- *Sea glass balls:* These glass fisher floats, which are sometimes quite old, are usually hand-blown glass balls that can be found washed up on shore. Today, you can find them for purchase in stores, but I suggest bringing store-bought balls to the sea and consecrating them with ocean water. These are sometimes also called witches' balls, and are often hung in windows and around the home to trap negative energies. They can be used as talismans to protect against the evil eye, especially if they are blue.

- *Sharks' teeth:* These amazingly powerful talismans can be used in protection and magic that needs a bit more aggression. Fossil shark or megalodon teeth radiate a more ancient power.

- *Shells:* Shells of all kinds have a wide range of magical uses.

- *Stones and fossils:* River rocks or other stones can be used in magic as an earth element. Crystals have many uses and, in folk magic, hagstones were highly prized. You can find these in river beds and at the sea shore. In addition, ammonite, belemnite, and other fossils that are associated with water or found on the shore are prized possessions of water witches.

- *Wands:* Driftwood or trees from the banks of rivers and streams are the ideal material for making a water witch's wand. These can be left plain or be lightly sanded, or they can be decorated with runes or sigils. The wand is a witch's tool for directing energy. Some sea witches choose to use a marlin spike to align with both the athame and nautical energies.

Exercise: Water Glyph Meditation

Now that you have a general understanding of water magic and some of its basic tools and practices, it is time to begin attuning your energy with that of water. Start by gathering drinkable water in a sacred vessel. Place this vessel in your lap or on your working space. Ground yourself (see chapter 2) and sit in front of your newly created and consecrated altar. Read through this visualization a few times to become familiar with it. Then close your eyes and complete the visualization.

Sit facing your altar; then take your hands and make the alchemical glyph for water. You can do this by placing your thumbs together and touching at the tip. Place your index fingers together, touching at their tips and pointing down, then curl your pinkie, middle, and ring fingers together into a fist. This will create a downward-facing triangle that, throughout the Western Mystery Tradition, is used as the alchemical symbol for water.

Once your hands are in position, close your eyes and begin to visualize water—your favorite body of water, rain, or a bath. Let your mind wander for a while and let the spirits guide you across different bodies of water—lakes, oceans, rivers, or streams.

Once you feel as if you have a strong image and feeling of the water, hold that vision in your mind. Visualize the water crashing over you and cleansing you. Visualize your heart center being cleansed of heavy burdens. Visualize the water washing over your body, covering all of you.

When you are done, let the water begin to swirl in front of you in your mind's eye. Let it create a floating, shining ball of water and let this shining ball start to form a downward-facing triangle—like the glyph you are making with your fingers. Make sure that the point is at the bottom. See this glyph in watery blue.

Holding this triangle in your mind, begin to connect with the water energy. Let the triskele symbol—the three-armed spiral (see Figure 1)—begin to form in the center of your triangle, each spiral representing water in one of its forms—liquid, gas, or solid. Let the triangle pulse and the triskele swirl in your mind's eye. Talk to the water; feel the water and try to feel what it is communicating to you. When you are finished, bring your focus back to the triangle. Ask if there is anything that water would like to teach you. Then wait and listen.

When you are finished, see the water glyph and triskele move toward the bowl of water in front of you. Let the watery glyph begin to pulsate on the surface of the water; let the triskele swirl. Let the glyph merge with the water in the vessel. It becomes small and then dissolves into it. When you are satisfied, slowly open your eyes, lift the bowl to your lips, and sip in the water that is now charged with the alchemical glyph. As you do this, allow your spirit to merge with the spirit of water and become one with it.

Chapter 2

River Witches

Rivers, like the ocean, are ever changing. They are constantly moving forward and ever flowing—eroding the earth beneath them, transforming their banks, and raging through the landscape. Rivers have long been associated with spirits and the Otherworld. Indeed, running water in general was considered sacred by the Druids, who thought that evil spirits could not cross it because of its holiness and purification properties. This belief may have come from the perception that, while the living could cross the water at bridges and fords, the dead could not, but had to be carried across. This, in turn, may have lent validity to the belief that evil spirits and ghosts could not cross running water.

Churches were often built near rivers and streams or by sacred wells—a throwback to Pagan days when water was sacred and associated with spirits and life. In faery lore, it is customary to cross a body of running water like a river or stream in order to escape an angry faery, a malevolent spirit, or a mischievous ghost. In Greek mythology, the River Styx served as the entrance to the Underworld. In order to cross it, you had to pay Charon, the ferry man, who brought you across to the other side. This belief also informed Roman practices, which, in turn, influenced Celtic practices as the Romans occupied Britain. In Celtic lore, Barinthus ferries those who wish to visit Avalon, crossing the water in his boat in order to access the Otherworld.

Folklore contains many beliefs and traditions that relate to running water. It was believed in some areas that fords and bridges, over which both the dead and living could pass, had magical or liminal powers. Any bargain made while standing over or in running water was considered indissoluble. Lovers who wanted to bring a solemn energy to their wedding vows stood on either side of a brook or river bank, dipped their fingers into the water, and held hands over it while saying their vows. Ritual processions often crossed a river or stream before performing a rite to indicate they had entered into sacred realms. Sitting on the bank of a river and tapping the soles of your feet on the surface of the water or circling them clockwise can aid in meditation and open a way into the Otherworld. In this chapter, we will explore some of this lore and then consider how it is used by water witches.

RIVER AND STREAMS

Folk customs, witches, and otherworldly beings have been associated with rivers in many ways throughout history. During the witch-trial era, witches were believed to be able to float, and so, in a trial by water, they were bound and thrown into rivers to see if they would drown. It was believed that certain rivers had magical properties, so water from these rivers was used for healing and protection. For example, an old folk cure for fever involved a new vessel, some salt, and water from three running brooks. Patients were instructed to drink from each brook and, after each sip, throw a handful of salt into it. At the first brook, they took a sip of water, then said: "Here is my head." At the second, they took a sip and said: "Here is my belly." At the third, they took a sip and commanded the fever into the water. It is important to note that, while traveling from one brook to another, patients were forbidden to look back or to speak, except to say the charm. It was believed that the fever remained in the water and didn't follow the patient home.

The direction in which a river or stream flowed often determined its magical properties. Water that flowed toward the sun was believed to have both healing and blessing properties. A stream formed from seasonal run-off in the month of March was considered lucky, and water gathered there was used in luck charms and spells. North-flowing rivers were deemed to be great places to deposit spells or to send messages to the Underworld. In Scotland, water from a south-running stream was considered to have healing properties. Fords were also considered places of healing and water gathered and used there was believed to have curative properties. People either washed themselves in the stream or drank from it, or sometimes dipped a shirt in the water and placed it on the one seeking the cure.

Rivers were also used in divination, shapeshifting, healing, and spell work. One such charm was used to foretell marriage. On All Hallow's Eve, a young girl dipped a shirt in the water where three rivers met, then took it home and hung it overnight on the fireplace mantel. If the charm worked, the figure of her future partner came and turned the shirt around to dry it on the other side. Likewise, alder trees were associated with rivers and seen as guardians protecting the water and the local water spirits that dwelled near.

Rivers were also used in various types of spell work, including rites for purification and cursing. To curse someone who has done you wrong, make a poppet of clay and place it in a river or stream with the head facing the current. Folk custom has it that, as the clay disintegrates in the water, so does the health of the person you are cursing. To break the spell, remove the poppet before it dissolves completely. Another old Scottish spell was used for both shapeshifting and for seeking justice. To perform the spell, a person rose at dawn, went to a place where three rivers merged, and faced east toward the rising sun. When the sun touched the water, the person drank a handful of water taken from that spot, then washed his or her face while reciting an old charm that speaks of the Holy Mother Mary, which was a name or epithet that referred to the White Lady or to other faery women (see chapter 3). The charm, which has Pagan roots, is found in the *Carmine Gadelica*, a book of prayers and incantations that preserved Celtic verse by hiding it in plain view among rewritten Christian liturgy.

RIVER SPIRITS

Stories of river spirits, nymphs, and goddesses abound in the Celtic tradition and local spirits inhabit rivers, streams, and canals all over the world. These bodies of running water flow all over the globe like an intricate web, connecting distant parts of the planet. Here are the stories of just a few of the spirits that inhabit them:

- *Bean-Nighe:* known as the Washer at the Ford in Scottish lore. This spirit washes the blood-stained clothes of those about to die. Fords and crossings where the water is shallow enough to wade through were known as liminal places and associated with crossroads. Thus they were seen as portals or bridges to the Otherworld. The Bean-Nighe was an omen of death sometimes associated with the Irish

Morrigan. It is said that any human bold enough to approach her and suckle at her breast can claim her as foster mother and ask that a wish be granted. She is described as a ghostly woman associated with death, midwifery, and the foretelling of misfortune and death in a family line or upon the battle field. Her cries and screams can be heard, carried upon the wind, by those who are about to die.

- *Boann:* the personification of the River Boann, or Boyne, in Ireland. She was also the lover of Dagda. Boann means "cow" or "divine cow," which gives her an interesting connection to faery cows and water bulls. Her story includes Nechtan (see chapter 8), who is associated with a well of wisdom surrounded by nine sacred hazel trees. The nuts from these trees that fall into the water are considered a source of wisdom. However, only Nechtan and his three cup or chalice bearers can safely draw water from this well. Boann comes into the story when she curiously approaches the well and draws water herself. The well begins to overflow, chasing Boann to the sea, thus creating the eponymous river. In some variations of the story, she was turned into a salmon, a fish associated with wisdom that is found in that river. She is also connected with, or actually may be, Modron and Rhiannon from Welsh mythology. She may also be connected with Brigid.

- *Danu:* considered to be an Irish mother goddess and one of the oldest Celtic deities. Her name means "river," but she was also known under the names Danann, Anann, and Anu. In Wales, she is known as Don. She is associated with the Danube, which is named for her, and is thought to be, like Sabrina (see below), the personification of the river. She also has a curious connection to the Tuatha De' Dannan, which means "people of Danu," making her a Celtic river goddess.

- *Sabrina:* a Brythonic goddess, nymph, and historical figure. Sabrina, called Hafren in Wales, is the goddess of the River Severn, which is the largest river in the UK. A mix of folklore surrounds her. Some believe that she is both a nymph and a goddess of the river. However, literature tells us that she was a Brythonic princess, daughter of King Locrin and Gwendolen, a Cornish princess. Locrin is said to have been forced to marry Gwendolen and, when his father-in-law died, he is reported to have thrown her into the river, along with Hafren. This may be when she became the nymph known as Sabrina. We do know from an account in the *Historia Regum Britanniae* that Hafren was, in fact, a princess and daughter of King Locrin who drowned in the River Severn. Milton mentions that wreaths of pink pansies and daffodils were given to Sabrina as offerings.

- *River Daughters of Plynlimon:* the three daughters of Plynlimon, a mountain spirit, who were associated with the rivers Severn, Wye, and Ystwyth. Named Vaga, Habren, and Aberystwyth, they were born of mist and grew into these three rivers.

- *Belisama:* a spirit associated with both rivers and lakes, and considered to be a water and solar goddess. She was the consort to Belenos and her name means "Bright One," giving her a solar aspect also associated with Belenos. The Romans referred to her as Minerva and so she joins the other fire/solar goddesses associated with sacred water sites like Brigid and Sulis, whom the Romans also equated with Minerva.

The river closest to where you live may not have a popular goddess associated with it, but that's no reason to ignore its power. Each river has a spirit or spirits of its own. The river itself may be home to a single entity, or there may be a host of water nymphs that dwell within its rapids or its gentle flow. Indeed, some rivers are considered to be the Titans who helped shape the earth. Each body of water has its own energy. Some may exert a dark and mysterious power; others may have clear healing properties. No matter what type your river may be, get to know the local spirits that live there. This will not only benefit you as a witch, it will also honor the river and the spirits that live within.

Exercise: Aligning with a River Spirit

For this exercise find a river, stream, or canal that is close to your home. This should be a place that you can visit often, or on a semi-regular basis at least. You can use a map or a GPS to find the best location if necessary. Be sure to check the water quality of the river; find out if the water is safe to swim in. If it isn't, either find one that is safer or modify this ritual to suit your needs.

Find a good time to visit the area. I recommend visiting on a Full Moon and when there aren't a lot of people around, so that you can have a quiet time with the river and not be disturbed. Bring a blanket with you, as well as a vial or bottle with a lid to collect water and a trash bag to collect any litter or debris. Gathering trash acts as an offering to the river and shows the spirits there that you are interested in helping the water. It demonstrates that you care for the spirits that live there, and are not there just to take and destroy as many humans do. You can also bring a tumbled, undyed, ethically mined healing crystal or stone to give as an offering.

When you arrive at the river, find a quiet place where you are safe and won't be disturbed, but one that is still close to the riverbank. Lay down your blanket and your other belongings. Scan the riverbank for any litter or debris that you can collect and remove to honor the water. This also gives you time to walk around and get to know the area. Connect with the plants that grow along the banks; feel the water with your fingers and notice the birds that fly around. When you are finished picking up litter, tie off the bag and place it in a trash can or carry it home with you.

Return to your blanket and find a comfortable position. Personally, I meditate best while lying down, but the important thing is that your position not distract you or keep you from entering a meditative state or a ritual mindset. Make sure you place yourself so that you have a clear path to the water. Remove your shoes and socks, and bare your legs to your knees if possible.

When you have found a comfortable position, breathe rhythmically until you reach a light altered state of consciousness. You don't want to be so deep into meditation that you fall asleep or are unable to keep your body safe around the water. Also, make sure you are grounded. When you have achieved a light meditative state, sit or stand so that you can begin to sway gently back and forth. Watch the rhythm of the water as it laps on the banks and match your swaying to its rhythm.

Keeping your eyes on the water, begin to move slowly toward the river. Raise your hands and gently hold them over the water as you step into it up to your ankles. Stop and continue to sway in rhythm with the river.

Begin to feel the energy of the river with your hands and body. Call out to it in your heart and mind, and with a strong voice. Keep it simple at first, only expressing your contact with and opening up to the river. If you wish, you can kneel down in the water or walk farther out. When you feel you have a good connection with the water, speak these words aloud:

> This child of water seeks to know you!
> I know to seek, I seek to know
> Where and how the river ebbs and flows.
> How the moon feels upon your dark waters and
> How the sun dances across your rapids.
> I seek to know the spirit of this river,
> And the spirits that dwell here.

Pause and wait. You can return to your blanket if you want to, and just sit and watch the water flow by. Pay attention to your surroundings and look for a sign. This may be a water bird dipping down in front of you, or a fish flipping out of the water, or even a glimpse of a river mermaid or nixie. If you don't see anything with your physical eyes, try closing them and looking with your mind's eye. You may also feel a sense of knowing or certain physical sensations that give you a hint of the water spirits' presence.

When you are satisfied with the communion, take your bottle and any offerings you have brought and approach the water again. Tell the water and the spirits that you are taking a vial of water to place on your altar to charge it with positive intent. Promise that you will return it, perhaps on the next Full Moon, after it has been charged, prayed over, and enchanted. Give the last of your offerings and return home without looking back.

Be sure to follow up and return the vial of water as promised. This will help connect you to the water and the spirits that dwell there, and show those that live in this area that you are committed to forging a relationship with them. It shows that you will honor them and revere the land.

If you are homebound, try using Google Earth to get a satellite view of a river and follow it from start to finish in a light meditative state, calling to the river using the words above and visualizing yourself there. This ritual can be performed with any body of water in which it is safe to swim.

CANALS, GHOSTS, AND DARK WATERS

Canals are manmade waterways that are similar to rivers and streams in that they embody movement and passage. During the Industrial Revolution, a canal system was created in England to carry goods and materials. These waterways often intersected and flowed from place to place under bridges, through dark tunnels, across aqueducts, and up and down through mechanical locks. While canals are relatively new waterways compared to ancient rivers and streams, they still hold mystery, as well as many restless spirits and ghosts. Moreover, canals are not limited to those built during the Industrial Revolution. Many canals were created, both before and after that, to help drain and irrigate the land.

Canals were frequently the site of gruesome murders, mysterious disappearances, and less-than-friendly poltergeists, perhaps due to their secluded locations. When working with the spirits of a canal, be sure to begin by researching its history and exploring old folktales and ghost stories to gain an idea of what took place there in the past. If it is a site of murders or kidnappings, or has a history of harmful energy, avoid it and find another—at least in the beginning. A skilled witch may be drawn to necromantic work or to helping lost spirits pass through the veil, but beginners had best beware—unless, of course, you are seeking out the practice for a specific purpose. Just be sure to protect yourself as best you can.

Once you have a solid history of the canal, begin to feel out its energies; try to identify stories or visions that weren't recorded in books. Remember that canals are usually associated with ghosts and human ancestral spirits, although there have been reports of spirited black dogs, White Ladies, phantom witches, and otherworldly creatures who have haunted their banks. You'll find numerous stories of dangerous deeds done on the banks of canals, as well as tales of witches and ancestral spirits who have haunted these waterways for one reason or another. Always use strong protection, at least until you get a feel for the canal and how benevolent its energy is.

Not all canal energy is baneful or deals with deathly sprits, however. During the Industrial Revolution, these waterways became the home of canal workers and their families, many of whom lived on the water in long boats called barges. Today, these are used primarily for holidays, although there are many indications that folk magic is still practiced on them. Many boats seen there today are adorned with Celtic knot work and popular moon and sun motifs. As in days of old, some still live a quiet nomadic life on the waters, perhaps providing charms, spells, and herbal remedies to those willing to bargain with modern-day witches.

GROUNDING AND SHIELDING

Once you have connected with the water and aligned with its spirit and energies, you must learn how to ground yourself, shield yourself from unwanted enemies, and protect yourself from aggression in both the mundane and spirit worlds.

Grounding is a process by which you align yourself with the stabilizing energies of the earth in order to keep a balanced and well-rounded energy. Even if you are an intermediate practitioner who is already familiar with this practice, it is always a good idea to go back to the basics. You are never too advanced to revisit foundational material and find value in it. Professional athletes don't refuse to walk because they know how to run. The same is true with magic; you don't forget the basics or refuse to revisit them just because you have been practicing more advanced magic. In fact, it is these foundational practices that give you the ability to explore advanced magic.

Since this book is about walking the path of water, or rather swimming down the river, we will explore grounding, shielding, and cleansing magic through a watery lens to give you a solid foundation on which you can build your practice. Grounding helps you remain present, calm, and collected as you navigate both shallow and deeper waters. In magic in general—but especially in water magic—emotions, feelings, and energies can creep up and dump down on you like a tidal wave. Common grounding techniques include hugging a tree, digging your toes into the dirt, or even visualizing roots growing out of your feet and into the earth to stablize you against these energies. While these are all wonderful techniques, there are several others you can use in conjunction with the water element that can benefit and ground you as you work with water energies.

Grounding

Watery people tend to be empathic. While this is not a set rule, it does seem to be the norm. Being an empath can be incredibly hard. Empaths sometimes feel the pain of the world all at once and can be overwhelmed by the energies of those around them. It can be hard for them to contain their emotions; like water itself, these emotions love to leak out all over the place, often in the form of tears, grief, or anger. I have noticed that watery-natured people connect and ground with water visualizations better than with earth-based practices like those involving tree roots and soil. Water-based grounding techniques help us manage our own watery natures better, letting us get a grip on our emotions, understand them, and flow with them rather than dumping them into the earth.

Below are some ideas on how to ground yourself for water magic, as well as an exercise to get you started.

- Dig your toes into the sand on the beach.

- Take a walk along the shore, giving your cares up to the ocean and the primordial Mother.

- Stand with your feet in water and connect to it.

- Take a bath with grounding or relaxing herbs.

- Drink a gemstone elixir made with a grounding stone like jasper.

- Work with ocean fossils and shells to ground and connect you to the earth element via the water.

- Lie in a bathtub or pool and let the weight of your body sink down to the bottom of the tub. (Be sure to hold your breath and don't stay there too long. Remember, breathing is essential for life!)

Grounding is an essential practice for any magical practitioner, no matter your path. It is the foundation on which to base the rest of your work. It keeps your energy balanced and in a good place to create magic; it helps you call on spirits and do ritual. Grounding can be done every day or just when needed, depending on who you are and how you practice—and, of course, on your own needs

Exercise: Grounding Bath with Drain Release

If you need something stronger than a bath in a gemstone elixir, which can be used every day for maintenance, consider taking a sacred grounding bath and using what I call the "drain release" to rid yourself of excess or negative energies. In this exercise, you will use a bath, herbs, and a special visualization to bring you to a balanced place.

Herbs that are roots, or from woody trees, are particularly well-suited for grounding work. My personal favorites are dandelion, sage, and valerian. In fact, all three together are delicious in a bath! Other good herbs for a grounding bath include peppermint, red rose petals, or catmint. And remember that some people react adversely to certain herbs or are allergic to them. Do not use herbs in a sacred bath that will irritate your skin, herbs to which you are allergic, or herbs that are considered poisonous. If you are unsure, it is always a good idea to consult your doctor first.

For this exercise, you will need a clean bathtub and a mixture of herbs similar to the ones mentioned above. You can sprinkle the herbs directly into the water or tuck them into a cotton sachet, like a tea bag, and let them infuse the water.

Begin by filling the tub with water. When the water is to your liking, place your hands over it and state your intent, clearly and loudly. Step into the tub and, if you have time, sit back and relax. Let your mind wander and think of the things that are keeping you from being grounded. Search your body for energies that feel discordant. In your mind's eye, notice and feel out your auric body and the energy and space that surrounds you. When you feel ready, stand up and pull the plug.

Take a few deep breaths. Now bring your attention to your physical body. Listen to and "look" at your body and energy. Look at your feet. Are they firmly planted? Or are you floating? Does your energy feel like static electricity from too much interaction with the digital world? Or is it like a hurricane whipping around all over? If yes, it is time to take control!

In your mind's eye, slowly gather this energy and bring it into your heart center. Imagine it forming a ball there. Begin to spin the ball around, cleansing it and bringing more unwanted energy into it. Continue this until you are satisfied. Then slowly let the ball slip down into your belly, down through your pelvis, and down your legs.

As you see the unwanted energy reach your feet, imagine that you are standing on an energetic drain, and that the drain is *free flowing* and not clogged. See the energy drip off your body and into the drain, going down into the earth where it is cleansed. Do this until your energy feels pure, harmonious, and where you want it to be.

To close, imagine the drain closing and disintegrating into the ground. Then see yourself reach up to the heavens, reaching with your arms in a V shape—like the alchemical symbol for water or a chalice. Let the heavens rain pure drops of crystal clear, positively charged water down on you. Let this cleansing water fall down and be caught in your "cup"—your V-shaped arms.

Allow your crown to open and receive this water. Let it fill all the places in your auric and physical bodies and replace all the negative energy that you just removed. When you are replenished with the waters from heaven, bring your hands together in a prayer position and touch your brow, then your lips, then your heart center. Thank the spirits you work with and thank the water. When the visualization is finished and the water has drained, be sure to close up both the visualized and the physical drains.

The herbs you use provide additional grounding properties to this rite. If need be, however, you can do this whole exercise in the bath with just water. In fact, in an emergency, you can use this visualization without any physical water at all—anytime or anywhere! As watery people, our emotions are fluid, and we often pick up on the vibrations and emotions of others. You may someday need to use this technique immediately and not be able to wait until you get home where you can draw a bath and relax.

Shielding

Shielding is a way to protect yourself from energies that are not your own, including energies in the astral realms. Although this is another practice that is considered a basic skill, even the most advanced practitioners work on their shielding skills often. Over time, shielding will become very easy for you. But remember: just because it is easy doesn't mean it is unnecessary. Shielding in the astral realm helps you maintain your ground connection and also helps you control the flow of energy you want connecting to you. It closes the door in the face of an unwanted guest and gives instant protection from unwanted astral entities.

Physical protection charms are made to protect you in the mundane and spirit realms or when you are unable to protect yourself in the astral realm (see chapter 3). In these exercises, you will use visualization. Find a comfortable position and enter a light meditation. When you have secured these visualizations in your mind, you can do them anytime, anywhere. When you have mastered the techniques, you may even be able to use them while conversing with a friend or an unwanted person.

Exercise: The Waterfall

The waterfall is a lovely technique I have been using for years. This is a particularly good technique to use when you want to interact with other energies but still want to guard yourself. For this visualization, start by seeing yourself standing behind a waterfall with the person or persons you are interacting with on the other side. The water flows continually, constantly cleansing the energy between you, as well as providing a barrier. This can be effective in a crowd as well; just visualize the waterfall all around you. You can speed up and increase the water flow if you need more protection, and ease up when you don't feel the need for such a strong shield.

Exercise: The Protective Bubble

The protective bubble is one of the most popular techniques and there are many versions of it. Some visualize a bubble; some visualize a ball of light. I've even visualized a ball of thorns! If you want to connect with the element of water while you shield, however, visualize a ball of clear water that is constantly swirling around you. This is also a good practice with which to start the day. Visualize yourself floating in a bubble that creates a watery cocoon around you. Do not dissolve the bubble before ending the visualization, so you can keep the protection constant throughout the day.

Spot shielding is a technique you can use to shield yourself immediately for urgent situations. You can do this using your mind's eye, even while you perform other daily tasks. Don't take the time to sit and alter your consciousness. Just begin your visualization to invoke immediate protection.

Exercise: The Ice Wall

The ice wall is one of my favorite shielding techniques. It works quickly and is more aggressive than the bubble or waterfall. In situations where your boundaries have been crossed, you feel unsafe, or you come into contact with an unwanted human or spirit entity, this can be useful. It also helps when you are dealing with an aggressive personality who doesn't take no for an answer.

In this technique, you visualize a block of ice falling from the heavens and landing right between you and whatever you need to shield against. The block can be as thick as you like; mine is usually a good two to three feet thick, depending on the circumstance. You can also surround yourself with an ice "box" in cases where the unwanted energy is hitting you from all angles. Be sure to melt this down after using it, however, so that you can connect with those you love and care for.

Exercise: The Tidal Wave

The tidal wave is used in emergency situations. We have all been caught in unexpected situations from which we need to escape or from which we need to protect ourselves. The tidal wave is an emergency shielding technique you can use to wash away anything you do not want in your sphere. To start, visualize a tidal wave that comes crashing in fast and furiously to clear out the unwanted person or energies. In some cases, you may also want the wave to wash away the disagreeable spirit or person completely. I usually visualize the tidal wave coming from behind the entity or person and washing them away, leaving my space and sphere clean and clear of unwanted energies.

CLEANSING AND PURIFICATION

Cleansing and purification are a necessary part of daily witch life. Like grounding and shielding, they are the foundation of our craft, but we are never too advanced to practice them. Cleansing and purification are often used together to rid you of impurities, attached entities, and funky energy, while raising your vibrations to a more pure, sacred, or holy state. Just as your physical body needs daily cleansing in a shower or bath to rid you of the impurities of your environment and daily work, so does your energetic body. Residual energy can build up while you are out in the everyday world, just as spiritual and energetic residue can build up in your ritual work. I personally tend to pick up negative energies at the grocery store; you may pick them up from work, from someone casting the evil eye at you, or even from a little slander or gossip that may have been sent your way. Cleansing and purification techniques can also be used to remove electromagnetic energy that builds up from the daily use of electronics and the unbalanced energy they can bring.

Here, we will focus on some basic techniques, but it is important to note that cleansing and purification are often used in conjunction with banishing and curse removals. Once the heavy work of these rituals is done, cleansing helps to remove the residual energy and purification helps to return you to a state of sacredness and balance. Developing a daily or weekly cleansing and purification ritual can be incredibly beneficial for all practitioners

Here is a list of herbs that are commonly used for cleansing and purification:

- Vervian
- Hyssop
- Basil
- White rose
- Birch
- Rosemary
- Peppermint
- Angelica
- Bay laurel
- Blessed thistle

We don't always have time to take a sacred bath or even to spend time in ritual or meditation. During these times, however, you can still connect with water and cleanse or purify by doing small things here and there to keep yourself aligned with your highest good. Quick ways to cleanse and purify include drinking holy or sacred water, spraying premade herbal purification mixtures or holy water, asperging, or saining with sacred herbs and holy water. On Beltain or Lammas, it was a traditional practice to sain the house and door post with straw in a sunwise direction.

Cleansing

Across space and time, water has been used by many cultures to purify, cleanse, and spiritually transform. The ancients knew that water was precious, and they treated it accordingly. In modern times, some countries have even given human rights to rivers. Unfortunately, others destroy them with pollution and contaminants. Ancient people and the generations that came after honored the practice of spiritual cleansing with water. Bathing, sprinkling, pouring, aspersing, and saining are all techniques that have been used to consecrate and spiritually cleanse across the ages.

Nearly all cultures have some type of cleansing ritual that uses water. Cleansing floor washes have been used by many folk practitioners. In Bali, high priestesses perform ecstatic cleansing rites by throwing water on participants as they chant and pray. In Hindu ritual, purification is practiced by bathing in the holy waters of the Ganges; those who practice Shintoism often use the power of a natural waterfall to purify themselves ritually. Hidden within Celtic and European mythology and folklore are remnants of similar practices that center around sacred wells, rivers, and lochs.

Water witches cleanse with water in a variety of ways:

- *Asperging with herbs:* Gather sacred, freshly picked herbs into a bundle, dip them in holy water, then sprinkle the water over the person, room, or item to be cleansed while praying, chanting, or intoning incantations.

- *Saining:* This is an old Scottish way of ritual purification. One method involved sprinkling or flinging holy water held in a vessel over the person or item being purified.

- *Bathing:* Take a ritual bath in water that has been blessed, consecrated, and made holy, or that has a tiny bit of salt in it to purify it. The grounding bath described earlier is also an example of a cleansing bath.

- *Floor washes:* Use these to purify a sacred temple, home, or other space. Ritual cleansing and purification are not limited to people. It can also be used to purify a physical location like your home or ritual space.

- *Spraying:* Add holy water to any spray bottle and use it in a more modern fashion to purify and cleanse.

- *River bathing:* Sit in a river to cleanse yourself of negative energies. Safely wade out to the center of the river and sit or stand with your back facing the direction of the water flow. As the water washes over your body, see the impurities that are taken away with it, and feel your energy being renewed.

- *Ocean bathing:* Let ocean waves wash over you to get the same purifying results obtained through river bathing. For both river and ocean bathing, exercise caution and stay safe!

Water Blessings

A water blessing is a ritual technique in which practitioners use sacred water to consecrate or bless (make holy) an object or person. The Scots call this *saining* ("to make holy"), and it is often done with sprigs of herbs.

Water blessings can be anything from a sacred cleansing of your bath space, to anointing your brow in ritual. You can also perform monthly cleansings of your shrines or sacred spaces. Or you may prepare a special offering or blessing for your water source and perform a regular ritual on its banks or shore. If you garden, why not water your plants with a monthly dose of gemstone elixir to promote extra growth and magic? Or sain the garden every quarter moon or during the waning moon. There are really many different possibilities.

Water blessings require a sacred vessel, sacred water, and a delivery method. This can be a small hand-held broom made of natural fibers, bunches of herbs from a garden, bundles of fresh culinary herbs found at your local grocery store, flowers you have picked and bundled together, a feather, a wand, or even just your own clean hands. You can even use bundles of grass or a leafy branch from a tree.

Your sacred vessel can be anything you like—a chalice, a glass bowl, or a special sacred bowl. I've given you some options for how to create sacred and magical waters; choose one of these and pour the water into the vessel. Say any incantations or prayers you like and set your intent. Take your bundle of herbs and dip them head-first into the water. Raise them out of the water and give the bundle a good flick, flinging the water in the direction of the area or object you want to bless.

Using water to bless or cleanse objects, yourself, or others is a great alternative to smudging. Though I love to smudge, smudging uses smoke and fire to cleanse and purify. As water witches, we can use water in the same manner. Note, however, that water can do more physical damage than smoke, so, in some situations, you may choose to smudge instead.

Exercise: Sacred Water Blessing

Select your sacred water and pour it into your sacred vessel. I recommend using a bowl, as it is bigger than a chalice and can easily hold a bundle of herbs. Once the water is in the bowl, gather your fresh herb bundle, wand, feather, or other implement and move to the space in which you are going to perform the ritual. If you want to say a blessing, prayer, or incantation, now is a great time. As you do so, project it into the water. When you are ready, dip the herbs into the bowl and fling the water in the target's direction, saying:

I cleanse this space
With sacred love and grace.
I banish all bane from this place
With the power of river, lake, and sea.
This is my will; So mote it be!

Exercise: Waning Moon Cleansing

During the waning moon, plan on ritually cleansing your bath, altar, or shrine. Pick one of the methods found in this book to create sacred water and select your broom, branch, or bundle of herbs. You can also bind wild flowers in a bundle. Use different methods each month and begin to make this part of your regular magical practice. Keep in mind that the cleansing is both physical and spiritual!

Exercise: Crystal Spray

You can make sacred water, pour it into a spray bottle, and spray it on the person, object, or space you want to cleanse instead of sprinkling it around. This is a great option for a more controlled ritual or even a daily saining. Find a good-sized spray bottle that is clean and ready for use. Place an amethyst or other gemstones into the bottle with the water. Put on the lid and let the water sit under the Full Moon to charge. Then spray the charged water wherever you need cleansing. See chapter 9 for more options and suggestions.

Exercise: Herbal Spray

If you are unable to burn incense in an apartment due to restrictions, or have asthma, or just prefer to use water-based materials, herbal sprays may be the solution for you. They are really fun to make and easy to use. All you need to do is gather your plant material, boil it in some water, and strain it out. Add a preservative like brandy or vodka and a few drops of an essential oil. Place the mixture in a spray bottle and let it cool. I suggest using hyssop, basil, or vervain.

Exercise: A Quick Daily Herbal Asperge

A really good way to cleanse quickly, or as part of a morning or daily practice, is to create holy water and sprinkle just a little of it over your body. Or you can use a bundle of fresh herbs from your garden to asperge your workspace, your temple, or your office. Garden herbs like rosemary and mint, as well as more exotic herbs like mugwort and wormwood—or even the branches of a fir or cedar tree—can be particularly effective and can bring the spirit and correspondences of the plant to the practice as well. Asperging your altar or sacred space is quite effective when done as part of a daily practice. It can help to keep the energy of your body and space in a balanced and holy vibration.

Purification

Purification is the process of making yourself pure. While similar to cleansing, its purpose is more to make you holy than it is to remove unwanted energies. I personally use cleansing to remove negative energies and purification to bring myself to a holy or sacred place. This is particularly useful before performing spells, rituals, and devotions. Purification has nothing to do with sin or being dirty. Rather, it has to do with restoration and the removal of energies that do not serve your higher good. It may even involve banishing a spirit that is hanging around and may not wish to leave. Of course, I use the two together, as you must first be cleansed in order to be purified and made sacred.

I use purification during ritual baths that I take in preparation for a working or that are meant to cleanse the body and purify the soul. Purification rituals are a little bit more complicated and require more work than a quick daily cleansing ritual. For this reason, I do monthly purification bath rituals in conjunction with the Full Moon.

Exercise: Full Moon Purification Bath

To prepare this bath, you will need:

- 1 pinch vervain
- 2 pinches hyssop
- 3 pinches ground white rose petals
- 1 tsp baking soda

- 1 cup Epsom salts
- 1 pinch sea salt

Under a Full Moon, combine your ingredients into a sacred vessel that has been cleansed and consecrated. As you place each ingredient into the vessel, pray over it, asking your deity or spirits to bless them and make them holy. Place the vessel out under the Full Moon to charge.

When your herbs are fully charged, mix or grind them together into a single blend, stirring sunwise at least nine times. As you do so, visualize a pure white ball of light dancing over the herbs, making them holy and ready for purification. When you are finished, take your ingredients inside and fill your bathtub with water.

When your bath is ready, pour the herb mixture into the tub and stir the bath sunwise nine times while you chant the incantation below. When you are ready, get into the tub. Be sure the water touches your entire body, including your hair.

> Spirits of the waters deep,
> My humble soul cleanse and keep;
> Purify my body and soul;
> Remove impurities and make me whole.
> With the power of the lake,
> river, swamp, and sea,
> Make me holy; purify me!

Chapter 3

Sacred Well Witches

Springs, founts, and wells are all fresh water sources that flow forth from the ground and are either caught in small pools or flow to merge with other sources. Many older texts do not distinguish founts from springs or wells, as we see in the story of Melusine, in which a water spirit appears with her two sisters at a fount in the middle of a forest. Most likely, this was a natural spring thought to be connected to the faery realm and perhaps even a portal to the Otherworld. The fae would have been honored close to the source from which both the water spirits and the fount flowed. In many cases, people controlled water emanating from founts by creating stone basins to channel the water in the direction they wanted it to go. Fount water is usually drinkable, clear, and associated with a spirit or faery being, although there are exceptions, as we will see below.

Folklore, myths, and archeology all tell us that these sacred water places were venerated and worshipped by the ancients and regarded as mysterious places where faery women in white or black phantom dogs were spotted in the liminal hours. Sacred wells have long been—and still are—regarded worldwide as holy, as places of magic, mystery, and healing. They are well known for having spiritual connections, housing spirits, and being portals to the Otherworld. They were regarded as places of worship and change by the ancients. In Europe, and especially in the Celtic regions, sacred springs and holy wells have been documented as religious centers or associated with popular historic sites by those who once inhabited the surrounding areas. Throughout Europe and the British Isles, there are hundreds of known sacred wells, founts, and springs, and probably thousands more that have been lost to time.

Some of the most popular wells that have survived to modern times—though not all are in working order—are Brigid's Well in County Kildare, Ireland; the Chalice Well and the White Spring in Glastonbury; the temple of Sulis at Bath; Coventina's Well on Hadrian's Wall; and Madron's Well in Cornwall. Archeology currently tells us that many of these sacred watery places were well-established magical or religious sites long before the Roman occupation of Britain. The Romans enhanced, encouraged, and changed the well practices. Seneca suggested that: "Where a spring rises or a water flows, there ought we to build altars and offer sacrifices." Later, Christians procured these sites for their own worship, again changing the names and spirits associated with them. Many Pagan practices were, in fact, kept and used by the new religion. This is why so many wells that were once named for faery women now bear the names of saints—Saint Brigid, Saint Ann, and Saint Mary among them. Before these wells were renamed, many of them were called faery wells, or pin wells, a nod to the magical practices that took place there even up to modern times.

Two perfect examples of this are Coventina's Well and the Sulis Temple at Bath. What we see today at the popular museum in Bath are the Roman remains of a temple to Sulis. However, Sulis was not a Roman deity. This suggests that she was associated with the site before the Romans arrived and that they continued to worship her there, although changing her name from Sulis to Sulis-Minerva. Indeed, adding Minerva to the deity's name showed how important both the Romans and the local Celts believed her to be. The Romans usually changed the name of the genius loci, the local spirit, of a site; their keeping her name in this case was quite different from their usual practice.

Wells and springs—unlike the ocean, rivers, or deep lochs—have a strange habit of appearing and disappearing at will. This is still true today. I once met a woman who, through dream work, found a well in the forest that had been lost over time. She was able to uncover it and clean it up. Likewise, many wells and springs dry up every year, and many more are lost to the mists of time.

Many of the springs across the British Isles are associated with healing everything from sore eyes to rickets, leprosy, and all manner of other diseases. We now know that some of this can be attributed to the different minerals contained in the spring waters and other properties found in natural springs. As magical practitioners, we also know that disease is sometimes caused by imbalances in the body, or curses, or negative energy, as well as by viruses or bacteria. It is important to note, however, that, although healing well traditions can enhance modern medicine, they in no way take its place. Always work with your doctor. On the other hand, I believe, as a witch and healer, that magic is incredibly useful and that there is no reason not to stack the deck in your own favor. Some of these wells and founts are known to ward off disease and I see no reason not to invoke their protection.

One spring in Shetland has a darker tale to tell. The spring, named Heljabriin, was known for its curative properties. A wandering peddler was murdered and then thrown into the spring. While you may think this would encourage the water to have more cursing properties, in fact just the opposite happened. It became even better known for its curative properties and many people went on pilgrimage to partake of its healing water. They traditionally dropped three white stones or coins into the spring as an offering.

Many sacred well traditions involve well dressings, votive offerings, clooties (or clouties, see page 100), cursing, healings, and prophecy. The Romans left abundant evidence of some of these traditions—artifacts like healing requests, curse tablets, and votive offerings. One of the most important and richest troves of votive offerings was found at Coventina's Well in 1878 in Carrawbrough, Northumberland. Coventina was a Roman goddess worshipped by soldiers stationed along Hadrian's Wall. The archeological site revealed twenty-four different Roman altars, along with votive tablets and offerings like coins, rings, beads, brooches, skulls, and other items. Well priests, spring priestesses, well tenders, cunning men, and wise women were all associated with these sites, with specific responsibilities to tend the wells, perform healing rites, or invoke curses for a fee. Evidence of these well and spring clergy persists today.

SAINTS AND WELL SPIRITS

When Christians built their churches atop old Pagan sites and by rivers named after ancient goddesses, they merely adapted Pagan well traditions of nymphs, water spirits, and gods who resided in the wells by dedicating them to saints. But the spirits, nymphs, and gods did not leave, so the spiritual and magical significance of the sacred wells was never lost. In fact, it is one of the few Pagan traditions that survive today. Water spirits have a habit of hoarding their treasures, and they have left us a wealth of evidence of their existence and their vast following around the globe, surviving in temples, as arti-facts, and in religions.

Christians rededicated Pagan wells to honor saints like Saint Sidwell, Saint Hilda, Saint Keyne, and Saint Brigid. Today, Saint Brigid's Well in Kildare, Ireland, is a very popular sacred well in the UK, although Brigid is honored at many such wells throughout Ireland. Brigid is special case, however, in that she is worshipped and revered as both a Christian saint and a Pagan goddess. And she is venerated in Scotland as well. One old charm survives in which figwort picked during a rising tide was used to protect cattle from the evil eye and help them produce a good flow of milk:

> I pick thee, figwort!
> For you contain blessed virtues;
> With these nine parts, nine blessings will come.
> By the blessing and virtue of figwort,
> Saint Bride [Saint Brigid] be with
>   me and guide my hand;
> I now pick you blessed figwort.

Well traditions also survived in the lore of cunning folk and wise women, who often attended church on Sunday morning and performed folk charms and rites the very next day. Wise women and cunning men knew the power of the springs and wells, and of the blessed waters the churches had often co-opted. They knew the power of religious objects that could be used in healing, including communion wafers, candle wax drippings, scrapings from religious statues, and, of course, holy water and water collected from holy wells found on or near church grounds.

We find evidence throughout folklore of wells being viewed as portals to the faery and to the Otherworld. The Brothers Grimm tell the tale of Mother Holda, or Holle, wherein a girl falls down a well after pricking her finger on a spindle. She passes through to the Otherworld, where Mother Holda lives among apple trees in a beautiful meadow. In the Celtic tale of the Horned Women (see chapter 1), the well itself speaks to the woman of the house, instructing her how to protect herself from the witches' enchantments. It is, indeed, significant that a traditional well is circular, mimicking the witches' sacred circle, mushroom faery rings, and the ancient stone circles, which were all portals to the Otherworld.

Groups of three and/or nine women are often associated with springs, appearing out of nowhere at a spring or well regarded as magical. In *The Nobel History of Lusignan*, first recorded in the 14th century by Jean d'Arras, Melusine and her two sisters appear out of nowhere at a fountain in the forest, indicating that it was a magical portal. While the shape of the fountain is not described, Melusine later casts a circle around a mountain, making a spring appear from the ground in a miraculous act. While this is not specifically described as a circle, she clearly creates a boundary that meets back at its starting point. Later, she presents gifts of magical rings. We see, in the case of the Glastonbury Chalice Well, that rings or circles are also used to illustrate magical and spiritual significance. While this is not made explicit in Melusine's story, it is an interesting correlation.

The modern definitions of "spring," "well," and "fount" are a little more precise than the historical and mythical usage. Springs are usually classified as large, fresh-water sources. They are also places to collect fresh water and often have a history of sacred usage by local or indigenous people. Wells, in the modern sense, are usually circular basins with a bucket or pump to haul water up from below the ground. Modern fountains are usually manmade, appear in commercial or civic settings, and have some type of mechanism that circulates the water. I usually work differently with modern fountains than I do with ancient founts. I have found that there are a few that do have local spirits, but they hold a different energy—one of pure joy and visual pleasure. Modern fountains are the living embodiment of water art and are, in themselves, a creation of beauty.

Modern wells and fountains are often associated with wishing. In a way, they receive votive offerings of coins, just as the springs of old did. Many throw a coin into the water hoping to have a wish granted—a throwback to old customs and bargains made with faery women at the site of an enchanted fount in the forest.

Exploring the famous sacred springs and magical wells found in Celtic traditions can shed light on how we create our own modern water practices. I personally find it fascinating that water temples survive in Britain and Europe today. The preservation of so many wells and temples stands as proof that a water cult existed there—a cult whose practices have been preserved in the folk charms and antiquities uncovered by archeologists. I share some of these stories below in the hope that water witches and magicians may be inspired by the old spells, myths, and folklore to weave their own modern magical water practice.

Mother Shipton and the Dropping Well

Mother Shipton was a renowned prophetess who was born in a cave on a river in Knaresborough in England. She was born Ursula Southeil, the illegitimate child of a young orphan girl named Agatha who gave birth to her in a cave on the River Nidd in 1488 (fifteen years before Nostradamus). She married a carpenter named Toby Shipton and became one of England's most famous prophetesses.

Mother Shipton was not only a prophetess, however. I consider her to be a water witch. Ursula was born close to an ancient magical wishing well that could turn items to stone. Rumor had it that there was a terrible thunderstorm the night she was born, which brought deep rumbles, cracks in the ground, and the smell of sulfur to the air. At birth, she was incredibly misshapen. In fact, some believe that she is responsible for the "hag" look that is often associated with witches. She was among the earliest witches in England to be described as misshapen and possessing the stereotypical crooked fingers and long crooked nose.

Mother Shipton had a nasty reputation for taking revenge on anyone who said hateful things to her, taunted her, or played tricks on her. She also had it in for common thieves, and even waged war on noblemen and kings. Unfortunately, we have no record of any magic she may have performed; but we do have her prophecies, her reputation, and her history, from which we can easily conjecture that she was a water witch of sorts. No doubt she laid curses and performed healing magic in the same way that others did at that time, and she may have used water from the sacred water sources around her cave.

The water found in this area created a "dropping well," which contains clear water that flows slowly over a sharp ledge. The water at this well collected in the small dents above the well and flowed over and down into the pool. Though the water was very clear, over time, items placed into it turned to stone—into part of the landscape. This is the only well of this kind in England. For generations, superstition and mystery surrounded the well. Small animals, leaves, sticks, and other things that fell into it were turned to stone, with no reasonable explanation. Of course, witchcraft and magic were credited with the phenomenon. In 1630, the well was opened to the public and people have flocked to it ever since. After a while, like many other holy wells, it became known for its healing properties. In the 1600s, it was considered to provide miraculous cures for just about any ailment.

Today, we understand the science behind this mysterious place. We know that the water is saturated with minerals that cause objects to petrify. The water flows forth from an underground lake, seeping through the earth in what we call an aquifer. As this happens, it is saturated with high levels of sulphates, carbonates with chlorides, and silica, as well as traces of zinc, iron, manganese, and aluminum. In much the same way that stalagmites or stalactites are formed, the calcite in the water deposits small layers onto items left in it; over time, rock-like accretions build up.

Water from this well is considered to be incredibly powerful. It holds the power of luck, granting wishes, prophecy, and petrification. Water collected from a cave where stalactites and stalagmites are formed will have these same properties and can be used in a similar manner. Cave fish are also considered to be very lucky, and the water from a cave-fish pool is very magical as well. Don't remove the fish, however! Leave them there, along with a wish. Cave water was believed to bring strength, but those who found a fish in a cave were only thought lucky if they left a nail, a coin, or some other metal offering at the cave entrance. Otherwise, their lives would be in danger.

Close to these petrifying waters is a wishing well that has the same mineral properties. There is a long and still-active tradition of making wishes at this well. While it is true that Mother Shipton's dropping well is like none other, similar phenomena take place in other caves, like the cave called Peter's Paps in Kirkmaiden parish, Wigtownshire. Water from this well caught in the open mouth was believed to help with whooping cough.

Sulis Temple

The hot springs in Bath, England, are dedicated to the British goddess Sulis, whom the Romans called Sulis-Minerva. Her veneration predates the Roman occupation, but it was the Romans who built her temple, and the British aristocrats of the Regency and Victorian eras who preserved it. Today, you can visit the museum and tour her temple and the sacred baths that the Romans once used for healing and rejuvenation. A trove of artifacts was uncovered here, including coins, gems, and curse tablets.

Sulis was, and still is, associated with healing and with healing waters, although the etymology of her name is still a source of controversy today. Some believe it means "clear sight," while others think that it is associated with the sun and means "eye of the sun." Still others claim that it means "gap," and so she is often referred to as the Goddess of the Gap. This is interesting, as Sulis isn't really either an Underworld deity or an above-world deity. Thus she truly is the goddess of the gap, the place between—she is both here and there, in and out. This is also reflected in her dual nature as both a healing and cursing goddess. Her springs were well known for healing and rejuvenation, but when excavations were done there, more than a hundred curse tablets were found. Many were etched on lead and beseeched Sulis to curse those who had caused harm or stolen goods.

Chalice Well

Glastonbury's Chalice Well has a long history, dating back through both Christian and Pagan times. Christians claimed the well held the Holy Grail brought there by Joseph of Arimathea, the secret disciple who secured and buried the body of Jesus. This is why it is called Chalice Well, and why it has become a place associated with healing and feminine transformation. The well's waters originate several miles away, bubbling up from a spring in this sacred landscape. Both physical ailments and spiritual illnesses have been healed here, and the well has earned a reputation for magical healing deeply connected to Avalon and the mysteries of the local landscape. The water from the Chalice Well does not originate here, however; rather it originates miles away and springs up only feet away from the White Spring (see below).

The technical term for the red, iron-rich water found in Chalice Well is *chalybeate* water. While this may be the most popular "red" well, there are many other springs and water sources that leave these iron-rich deposits. In fact, there are literally hundreds of chalybeate springs worldwide. Even the Sulis spring at Bath leaves an orange tint where it flows from the earth.

Moreover, red wells are not the only colored water source. There are a few reports of wells containing black water. A sulfurous spring outside of Queen Camel in Somerset is said to turn silver black, thus earning it the name Blackwell. There is another curious black well, called King Arthur's Well, in south Cadbury. In the early 1900s, this well reportedly contained black water that may have been toxic. There is also a small, dark well in Glastonbury, within the depths of the abbey ruins in Lady Chapel. A small archway covers the stagnant well once used by the monks who lived there. This black well, lying so close to the White Spring and Chalice Well, brings an additional layer to the mysterius waters of Glastonbury.

The White Spring

Across from the famous Glastonbury Chalice Well, separated only by a narrow lane, lies a mysterious and dark sanctuary. This is the home of the White Spring, a temple dedicated to the deities Gwyn ap Nudd and Brigid. Here, in an old Victorian well house, candles light the walls and shrines; altars stand along the walls and in the corners. An archway of hazel branches frames a divine goddess figure and two carved dragons form an archway leading to Gwyn's shrine. The trickle of water is ever present. Outside the gates of the well house is a small shrine adorned by bits of ribbon, glass, and other glittering objects. The iron gates that open on to this dark sanctuary boast the symbols of Glastonbury—the sacred flame and Brigid's cross—and the energy of Morgan le Fay hangs heavy over both the shrine and the ancient town (see below).

Although in close proximity to it, the White Spring is not connected to Chalice Well in any physical way. They have completely different water sources. The White Spring derives its name from the limestone deposits that have built up along the path that the water that feeds it travels. This water is rich in calcium and has healing properties. The landscape is immersed in magic. Glastonbury Tor is the realm of the Faery King Gwyn ap Nudd, who is the ruler of Annwn and the sub-aqueous faery beings called Plant Annwn. The White Spring bubbles up at the base of the sacred hill before flowing toward Chalice Well, paralleling the path of that well's waters.

Saint Madron's Well

Madron, a Cornish saint, was a patron of healing and cures for whom a healing well in Cornwall was named. No documentation of Madron's life survives, but he may be a Christianization of the Welsh mother goddess, Modron. Modron, in turn, is often associated with Morgan Le Fay, famous sister of King Arthur, who was known as a great healer and protector of springs before her character was demonized by later Arthurian writers.

Sacred Well Witches

Morgan Le Fay was the chief of nine priestesses, as recorded in the twelfth century text *Vita Merlini*. As her name implies, she is a faery woman and many venerated her as a goddess. Her name means "sea born," so she is connected to and associated with more water sources than just wells. By linking Saint Madron to the goddess Modron, and then to Morgan Le Fay, however, we can posit a connection between this well and Morgan, and therefore classify it as a faery well.

Saint Madron's Well is located in Penzance and is still a very popular site. One curious tale of healing associated with the well tells of a man named John Trelill who had been disabled for sixteen years. In 1640, he bathed just once in the healing waters of the well and was cured.

Melusine's Fount

Melusine, sometimes called Melusina, has a long history, with many variations and even some seemingly unrelated accretions. I will do my best here to recount her tale as succinctly as I can.

Melusine was the oldest daughter of a Scottish King and a water nymph named Pressina. When Pressina married the king, she promised that, as long as he never looked upon her while giving birth, she would remain faithful and he would be rich. Pressina became pregnant with triplets and, when it came time for the birth, the king inadvertently entered the birthing chamber during the birth of the third and last daughter. Angry, Pressina

gathered her children—Melusine and her two sisters—
and left Scotland to live in Avalon. When the girls were
fifteen, they learned the story of their birth, and cursed
their father and turned him to stone. Pressina became
angry, for she still loved her husband dearly. She, in turn,
cursed her daughters, relegating the youngest to life in a
tower guarded by a flesh-eating hawk, condemning the
second to a life guarding her father's body, and proclaim-
ing that the oldest, Melusine, would spend each Satur-
day of her life with the tail of a mermaid—or in some
versions of her story, a serpent's tail.

The story picks up again at the Fount of Thirst when
Ramondin, a young man of noble blood who was riding
through the forest, happens upon Melusine and her two
companions. After a short teasing dialogue, Melusine
declares that she will marry him as long as he obeys her
and performs a series of strange tasks. She then gives
him two magical rings and sends him back to his home.
While performing his assigned tasks, Ramondin acquires
a large land holding which, when measured out by two
faery-like men, circled around a mountain and back to
where it began. At this spot, a magical fount sprang forth.
Melusine then married Ramondin in a beautiful faery
wedding complete with riches, tents, and much feasting.
Melusine and Ramondin lived together for many years
and had several children.

One day, learning of Melusine's habitual absence
on Saturdays, Ramondin's brother questioned her

faithfulness and challenged her husband to investigate. As Ramondin peeked through a keyhole in a door, he saw Melusine in her bath splashing her mermaid's tail! He guarded his wife's secret and banished his brother. Then a series of misfortunes began to plague the family. Their children began to go mad or were murdered. Ramondin, in his grief, cried out: "You demon woman, look what you have done." Melusine told him that she knew he had betrayed her, but would stay with him as long as he kept her secret. Unfortunately, he had already told others in his anger, so she sprouted dragon wings and jumped out the window, circling the castle three times before flying away. It is said that, when someone in Melusine's blood line is about to die, you can hear her shrieks and banshee cries foretelling their doom.

Melusine is a faery woman who is alleged to have human descendants. She is credited as the ancestress of various noble families including the Lusignans, a prominent French family whose scions include Guy de Lusignan, one of the Kings of Jeruslem. She was also said to have married Siegfried I, Count of Luxembourg. This family has strong ties to the War of the Roses through the Rivers family. Jacquetta of Luxembourg, also known as Lady Rivers, bore a daughter named Elizabeth Woodville, who became wife and queen consort to King Edward IV. Melusine's image persists today as the mer queen on the Starbucks logo.

TREES AND HOLY WELLS

Many different types of trees are associated with holy wells, and there is a substantial body of folklore and modern experience to support this. Some wells have had trees intentionally planted near them, like the thorn tree in Chibby Drine on the Isle of Man. Others have trees that grew naturally near or around them, often shielding them from easy view. And many of these trees have a folklore and sacred history of their own.

Besides bringing their unique energy and associations to the wells they surround, trees follow the general sacred-well themes of protection, healing, and association with water spirits. Some even believe that particular trees act as well guardians, housing the spirits that guard the wells and maintaining a mystical connection to them. Rags or clooties (see page 100) and votive offerings are often left in, on, or below the trees that are close to sacred wells. Here are some of the trees most commonly found in proximity to these wells.

- *Elder:* a faery tree that has also been associated with witches and enchantments. There are several wells from Roberttown in England to Wales that have elder trees growing in their landscape.

- *Ash:* sacred in both England and Scandinavia. In northern lore, Yggdrasil is a huge ash tree that connects the nine realms—although there is some speculation that it was actually a yew tree. At the foot of this great World Tree is the well of the past (Urth's Well), the well of wisdom (Mimir's Well), and the spirit well called Hvergelmir. Ash trees abound in the British sacred-well landscape. A few good examples are the Holy Ash Well, Peggy Well, Skye Well, and Saint Nun's Piskie Well.

- *Oak:* a tree with many types of folklore associated with it. It is sacred to many male deities like Zeus, Thor, and Yahweh. It was also strongly associated with the Druids. Wells that are associated with oak trees are Healy Well, Llancarfan Well, and Priestess Well. Oak was also associated with oracular work, portals, and wisdom.

- *Hazel:* a sacred tree associated with countering witchcraft, wand lore, and dowsing. The Well of Segais from Irish lore is said to have nine sacred hazel trees that hang over its waters; the nuts are said to confer wisdom on the salmon who swim in the pool and eat them. Hazel nuts have also been used as votive offerings. Branches from this tree were used to form the traditional forked sticks of dowsers, or water witches.

- *Holly:* another tree associated with protection. The Romans believed it was a healing tree and it was sacred to the Druids. There are many wells in Wales and England that have holly surrounding them and several in the UK as well, including Tomblig Well.

- *Yew:* associated with death divination, which was performed with yew branches. Many yews have been found growing in the sacred groves surrounding holy wells. There are at least six sacred wells in Wales that have yew planted near them. A famous well with yew trees is the Chalice Well in Glastonbury.

- *Rowan:* a tree with a long folk history associated with protection and divination. It has been found at many wells in the UK. Although the rowan doesn't have as strong a connection with sacred wells as trees like yew, hawthorn, and hazel, it still has a presence. It has a long history of being used to protect against witches and witchcraft. On May Day near Priest's Well, close to Narberth, children decorate wells with rowan to keep witches away.

- *Hawthorn:* long associated with protection magic and the faery realms. Thomas the Rhymer met the Faery Queen at a hawthorn tree, and it is considered a sacred tree in the Glastonbury revival practices. Lady Well, Hesp Well, Margaret Well, and other faery wells are often found surrounded by or near hawthorn. Hawthorn was associated with Beltain and charms were made from it to protect cattle and against sorcery. It is also associated with chastity, purification, and Avalon. Hawthorn is most famous for being a faery tree and hawthorn that stood alone near holy wells marked the place as sacred to those of the faery realm.

- *Alder:* not always associated with sacred wells, but always associated with water and water spirits. Alder was associated with protection and it was believed that alders that grew near sacred water sites, rivers, and streams acted as guardians or protectors of the water spirits that lived there. The cones from this tree, sometimes called black knobs, were used to decorate holy wells. Alder is another tree used in dowsing to find water. There are folk tales of water spirits being trapped in alders.

OTHER WELL GUARDIANS

In Scotland, wells were deeply connected to local deities and often had shrines or places of worship near them. They were seen to represent life and spirit, and each body of water was believed to have its own spirit or guardian. Other entities acted as guardians as well—black dogs, faery women, and phantoms. There was even a human skeleton found standing upright in one well shaft.

In the magical town of Glastonbury, many have reported that a woman in white, who is called the Lady of Avalon, walks the gardens around Chalice Well, appearing to those who are in need of her. In fact, "ghostly ladies in white" abound in the British Isles and are often associated with holy wells and marshes. And similar folk beliefs are found outside the British Isles as well. In fact, it was believed that every county and each well had such a spirit. Black dogs were also associated with water, and there are many folk tales and beliefs that place phantom-like black dogs in the liminal spaces between land and water.

MINERALS AND CHEMICALS

Springs and wells are known for their curative powers more than for anything else, and the image of a sacred well brings visions of healing to mind. And, as it turns out, there are scientific reasons behind some springs' healing properties. Thermal springs, or hot springs, like those found at the Sulis Temple at Bath were very popular as places of restoration and healing with aristocrats of 18th-century Britain. The United States has many warm or thermal springs that were, and are, used for therapeutic purposes. Spas grew up around them that became very popular as tourist sites in the late 19th and early 20th centuries. Some are still in operation today.

Besides the therapeutic properties of hot water, many springs and wells contain high levels of dissolved minerals that also have therapeutic properties. To the ancients, these minerals were unknown, but their effects were not. Some of the hidden minerals found in these sacred wells include arsenic, iron, radon gas, calcium, bicarbonates, sulfur, sodium chloride, and magnesium. Springs that contain sulfuric gas were considered to be healing springs. Because this gas has antibacterial and expectorant properties, bathing in warm sulfuric water helped relieve respiratory, digestive, urinary, skin, and venereal ailments.

Radon is an invisible, odorless radioactive element that manifests as a gas. It is considered to be a dangerous health hazard today. However, it also has a history of healing and prophecy. Radon gas is known to induce sleep and is reputed to encourage prophetic dreams. While today we know that radon can be harmful, in the past, it was part of the mystery of dreaming wells like Saint Madron's Well and Sancreed Well. Many visitors to these wells came deliberately in order to sleep and receive messages from the spirit world via prophetic dreams. There are cases where radon gas was (and is) used to treat rheumatism, skin disorders, blood-sugar disorders, gallstones, women's ailments, and respiratory issues. Please note: I do not recommend exposing yourself to radon gas for these purposes! Modern medicine has safer and more efficient treatments for them. However, if you need spiritual insight about these ailments, taking a rest near a well like Saint Madron's may bring clarity and set you on the path of healing.

Arsenic is another toxic mineral found in springs. However, in minute quantities, arsenic can have healing properties. That said: Don't expose yourself to arsenic!

Iron, calcium, and magnesium are also found in many wells around the world, Chalice Well and the White Spring among them. Magnesium is known to help with the body's regulatory functions and cellular processes, as well as to help muscles relax. Iron can help with anemia, mental fatigue, and nervous-system disorders. Calcium can help bones, liver, muscles, and heart, and can be used to treat digestive disorders.

Despite the science behind some of the healing and curative properties of well water, however, we must never lose sight of the spiritual and magical properties of these waters and their connection to the natural world. In herbalism, we know that herbs have compounds in them that give them healing powers, but we also invoke the spirit of the herbs and work with their magical as well as their medicinal properties. The same is true of water. Science may back up some of the curative properties of springs and wells, but much will be lost if we forget that these sacred waters have spiritual and magical powers as well.

Finally, a warning! Do not drink water that may contain high amounts of toxic minerals. You are responsible for researching your site and the water it provides, and for making wise decisions based on the results of your research. If you are ever unsure, do not drink the water unless you have established, beyond a shadow of a doubt, that it is safe for human consumption.

WELL CHARMS AND CUSTOMS

Since many customs involving sacred wells and springs were never really lost, and many were still being practiced into the 18th century and even into modern times, a good number of folk spells, healing charms, and curse tablets have been preserved. Below, we will look at some of these charms and consider modern interpretations of them that you can incorporate into your practice. While this chapter deals specifically with fresh-water springs and wells, clever witches can reasonably adapt any of these practices to their own sacred bodies of water— whether lakes, rivers, or perhaps even the ocean.

Chants, songs, herbs, stones, pins, and other objects are used in conjunction with holy or sacred wells to work charms. As we saw in Dr. Emoto's research, water holds the vibration or power of the chants, songs, and objects to which it is exposed. Our ancestors knew this. Folklorist Charles Godfrey Leland explained how certain healing and magical properties of herbs were thought to be increased and enhanced by combining them with or submerging them in water. The spirit and properties of the plant, stone, or object were simply transferred to the water. The spirit of earth passed into the plant and the spirit of the plant then passed into the water. Magicians, using song or chant or prayer, could then send pain or harmful energy back to its source through sympathetic magic.

There are thousands of folk rites and charms from almost every culture that involve a sacred body of water—rites that include adding plants or herbs to water and washing floors with it, bathing children and the sick, using stones dipped in water, or charms using waters directly to heal. All give us hints into how our ancestors practiced. These ancient charms provide inspiration to modern water witches when they use them to craft spells based on the old folk practices. Even the simple act of dropping coins into water as an offering or in exchange for a wish is quite an ancient practice that can be traced to pre-Roman times.

Wells have also been used for more sinister magical workings. In the case of the temple at Bath dedicated to Sulis, over 100 small lead tablets called *defixiones* were found that asked Sulis-Minerva to punish or curse people for various offenses, often for stealing clothing or other property while the victim was bathing. Wells with water that was undrinkable, sulfuric, or dirty were also used for cursing, although many other holy wells did their share of cursing, too. One popular curse involved bending a pin, possibly from the clothing of the person you wished to curse, or bending a pin while saying the person's name, then dropping it into the well—hence the term "pin well." In some cases, a well-tender, wise woman, or cunning folk was paid to create a charm or spell, either to curse an enemy or to heal.

Some wells have baneful spirits attached, and some spirits that may look malevolent really aren't. Several wells are known to have complete skeletons in them. In some cases, these were considered to be well guardians; in others, it was believed the skeletons were put there as a sacrifice or perhaps as a punishment. Sometimes, the spirit that dwells in the water is a lost soul that belongs in the realm of ghosts or ancestors.

In Chapel Wells, which is located in Kirkmaiden parish, there is a well that is believed to have curative properties. It is unique in that it is located near the sea and has three different basins or pools where sea water mingles with the water from the well when the tide comes in. In a charm recorded there, a child was stripped naked, held by one foot, and dipped in the first basin. This was repeated in the second basin. Finally, the child's face and eyes were washed in water from the third basin. To complete the rite, an offering was left in a chapel cave, specifically behind the western door. The rite was believed to heal sickess in the child

There is a well on Isle Maree in Loch Maree, Scotland (named after Saint Maol Rubha), where a charm was performed to heal mental illness by towing the patient three times around the island in a boat, dipping him or her into the loch after each circuit. After the third circuit, the patient drank water from the holy well on the island. Later, a clootie on a nail or a coin was driven into the tree by the well.

In Christian folklore, people approached some holy wells invoking the Trinity before circling them and then immersing themselves in the water for a cure. These wells were often dedicated to Saint Mary and were visited by women who had trouble conceiving. Well water was also often used for healing divination using a tub or bowl of water that was brought into the sick person's room. A wooden bowl was floated upon the well water in the tub. If the bowl moved clockwise, it was a favorable sign; if it moved counterclockwise, it was unfavorable.

Lady Wilde recorded a curious folk charm that involved a holy well. Nine black stones were gathered before sunrise. The person seeking a cure was led by a rope to the sacred well, taking care never to speak. Three of the stones were then cast into the well: the first in the name of God, the second in the name of Christ, and the third in the name of Mary. This was repeated on three consecutive mornings to cure the disease. This charm can also be performed in the name of the Faery King, the spirit of the well, and the Faery Queen.

The Lucky Well of Beothaig, near Kintyre in Scotland, had a reputation for being able to control the winds. To produce the desired wind, the well was cleaned out with a bowl or clam shell and the water was thrown in the desired direction three or nine times.

The pools of water over which bodies were carried to funerals, especially pools at a ford or a bridge, were often gathered to counteract the evil eye. This charm involved taking the water very carefully in a vessel that did not touch the ground, then dipping a wooden ladle that held a piece of silver into it. Finally, the person being treated drank three sips of the silvered water and was sprinkled with the remainder. Silvered water (see chapter 1) played a role in a number of these charms. In one case, the well was circled three times and the silver dropped into it. Then a wish was made while drinking the water, followed by an offering.

In Scotland, the first pail of water drawn from a well on New Year's Day brought good luck and would help secure a good mate. One curse based on an old Scottish charm directed the practitioner to extinguish a black candle with the target's name carved on it while saying:

> May all your meetings be bad.
> May you not grow well.
> May all you love fall to ruin.
> May you never understand.
> May harmful accidents happen to you.
> Black water, a curse upon you.

VOTIVE OFFERINGS

Holy wells are visited on a variety of different days for different reasons—sometimes for pilgrimage, sometimes to bring offerings, and sometimes to recognize or celebrate a particular deity or saint. In the latter case, the visit itself became part of the offering. In some cases, the day of the week on which the visit was made was important—sometimes on Sunday, or on the first Sunday of the month, or on consecutive Fridays. Sometimes specific dates determined the visit. For example, Saint Catherine's Well, located on the southern coast of the Isle of Eigg, was visited on April 15th by villagers who circled the well clockwise. The cross-quarter days of Beltaine (May Day), Samhain (All Hallows), and Imbolc (Candlemas) were popular days for visiting wells. During these special visits, the wells were often dressed with beautiful flowers, fruits, and candles as a means of giving offerings and thanking the spirits, whether saints, water nymphs, or fae.

Votive offerings were also given to pay for curses to be cast or for healings to be done. In this sense, they can be regarded as trades, or even bribes. Items used in these offerings include a wide range of artifacts, including clooties, stone carvings, human heads, sacrificed animals, weapons, cauldrons, gemstones, pins, curse tablets, beads, and jewelry.

FOSSILIZED AMMONITES

The fossilized remains of ancient sea creatures carry their own watery power, and some sacred well sites have incorporated them into their structures. Good examples of these are ammonites, which are the fossilized spiral-shaped shells of a type of mollusk that lived at the same time as the dinosaurs. Ammonites carry the primordial energy of the sea, but also have an interesting connection to wells and fresh water. They are ancestral and their shape can represent the cycles of the earth and the cyclical nature of the Craft. They can be used in ways similar to, or in conjunction with, the chambered nautilus, which is also spiral-shaped.

Ammonites were revered by our British, Greek, and Roman ancestors, as well as by our German and Scottish forebears. The Romans believed that placing a pyritized ammonite under your pillow induced prophetic dreams; the Greeks thought that placing an ammonite under your pillow cured insomnia and induced pleasant dreams. And it is likely these practices were brought to the Celtic world. This tells us that modern witches can use ammonites to aid in dream work, divination, and prophetic dreams.

Ammonites were sometimes called snake stones or draconites. In medieval Europe, they were believed to be petrified snakes and were often painted or carved with heads. They are associated with holy wells found at Glastonbury, Whitby, and Keynsham; they adorn the gardens at Chalice Well and line the beaches of Lyme Regis. They are associated with Saint Hilda, Saint Keyne, and Saint Cuthbert. The holy wells in Whitby and Saint Keyne both tell very similar stories about how these saints turned all the serpents in the land to stone. If you break open an ammonite, they claim, you will find a serpent inside. These beliefs and practices survived well into the Victorian era. It was quite common for cunning folk or others to carve a serpent's head onto an ammonite as "proof" of its serpent origins and to use the fossils to create charms.

In traditional folk magic and witchcraft, ammonites can be used as "stroking stones." Stroking stones are usually flat stones used for healing, but ammonites work very well for this purpose. Traditional charms have the practitioner stroking the stone over the body, healing an afflicted area by transferring the disease from the body into the stone. If the afflicted person is not available for the procedure, the body can be visualized and the stone stroked as if it were the afflicted body part. As in all folk magic, this charm can be used to both harm and heal. In the western islands of Scotland, ammonites are called "cramp stones," because it is believed that they can cure cramps in cows by washing the part affected with water in which the stone has been steeped for some hours.

In European folk magic, ammonites were used as fertility charms, as healing charms, and to create a healing water preparation. They were also placed in milking buckets to prevent the milk from drying up. Fisherman used them to ensure a good catch and sometimes wore them as pendants or rings. There is also written evidence that pyritized ammonite was carried as a good luck charm during the early 1900s.

You can make an ammonite gemstone elixir that you can use in your modern water magic. Just be careful not to ingest the water, as some fossils contain pyrite and can be toxic. You can charge the elixir with a specific intent while creating it, or use it for any of the traditional purposes discussed here—dream water, anti-cramp charms, and healing.

CLOOTIES

The word *clootie* comes from the Scottish word *cloot*, which means "strips of fabric." Clooties (or clouties) are torn rags, pieces of cloth, or clothing that are dipped in holy water and hung, tied, or nailed onto a sacred tree that stands near a sacred well. Sometimes taglocks like hair, blood, or spittle are used in addition to the rag, or on the rag as it is tied on the tree. If the tree is a hawthorn, the rags can be impaled upon a thorn rather than tied onto a branch.

Clooties have been used in a variety of ways at sacred wells. Traditionally, those who were hurt or in need of healing approached a healing well and tore a piece of fabric from their clothing close to the affected area. The rag was then dipped in the holy water—sometimes three times—as prayers or incantations were intoned, then either tied back onto the sick person, attached to a holy tree, or buried under a rock or near the well. If the rag was tied back onto the sick person, the holy water it contained was used to heal the affliction directly. When it was hung on a tree, it was believed that the tree took the illness or affliction away through transference. When it was buried, the rag decomposed and, in doing so, carried the illness away into the ground.

One old charm for healing a child has two older women accompanying a mother and child to a sacred well. Here, the mother dipped a chalice into the water and drank from it. Then one of the wise women dipped a rag in the water and wound it around the child's head, covering its eyes, while the other gathered additional water in a bottle.

Clooties are not only used for healing, however. They can also be used as votive offerings, although this seems to be a more modern practice. Such modern practices, while not ancient, can help to establish a ritual state of mind, and can add their own magic and energy to sacred sites. When used as a votive offering, the clootie can be dipped in the well, properly blessed, and hung in a tree as an offering for the spirit of the well, the well guardian, or the genius loci.

Never remove other people's clooties, rags, coins, or pins from sacred sites, because their troubles, illnesses, or negative energies could rub off on you!

Exercise: Clootie Charm

Choose a version of the clootie spell that appeals to you and perform it. Feel free to make up your own version; get creative! One caution: in modern practice, you must be careful to use only fabric that is biodegradable, like unbleached and undyed cotton, linen, or silk. Manmade fibers like polyester will not decompose and can pollute the sacred area; modern dyes can be toxic. Part of the magic is that, as the material decomposes, the illness or affliction diminishes. Using materials that do not decompose will defeat the power of the charm. If you don't have natural-fiber clothing that you wear often, buy a piece of cotton and tie it around the afflicted area for nine consecutive days to connect it with you and your affliction; then perform the rite at the holy well. This is a good modification and is better for the environment and spirits that surround the well.

Finally, if you visit a sacred well and want to personalize your clootie with blood, spit, or hair, be careful not to introduce your bodily fluids into popular sacred sites—and don't put them in the well!

Exercise: Entering the Faery Realm

Many folktales and mythologies describe sacred wells and springs as watery portals to the Otherworld. In this exercise, you will visualize a well and use the vision to access the Otherworld, the world of the faery.

Please note that you will be using the well to enter the Otherworld through spirit flight and not literally. *Do not actually jump into a well* as this can cause injury or worse. Always take precautions around water to be sure that you are safe. This meditation can be done either near a well—perhaps sitting by it—or in your home. You can also try it next to a river or the ocean, modifying the visualization to suit your needs.

To prepare, find the location you want to use. This can be in your temple room, by your altar, in your bathtub, at the beach, or while visiting a holy well or recreational spring. If you are working in your temple room or by your altar, consider adding holy water to a sacred vessel that you keep on your altar. Working through manmade fountains that connect to a series of pipes can sometimes be problematic, although they can have a powerful magic of their own.

Take a ritual cleansing bath before this journey. Relax, but don't fall asleep. Be sure to read through this visualization several times so you have a good idea of how the meditation flows as you begin to lead yourself through it. When you are finished, always, always, always be sure that you return the way you came and re-enter your own body. This meditation will lead you into the realm of faery; what happens there and where your path leads are up to you. Just remember when it is time to leave to retrace your steps back to your starting point in the field and stare back into the sun.

Next, connect with the water you are working with. Begin to breathe, focusing only on your breath. Just let any thoughts that come to mind pass you by. Bring your attention back to your breath. When you feel relaxed and your mind is clear, begin to count to nine, slowly and rhythmically, synchronizing with your breath. When you reach nine, let your mind wander around in the darkness. Look for a tiny pinprick of light anywhere; try to find that light and focus on it. Let the light grow bigger and brighter, until it is so bright that you have to turn away. As you do this, realize that the bright light is the sun. As you turn away, you see green grass all around you, with a forest off in the distance. You are standing among the tall grasses, with moon-like daisies with large yellow centers and white petals all around you, reaching up to the sun. Tall sprigs of vibrant pink foxglove surround you. Little bees buzz in and out of their leopard-print centers, legs covered in pollen; they dart in and out of the flowers and buzz all around you.

Begin to walk, exploring the field you are in. Feel the tall grasses brush against your legs and hear the birds chirp. In the distance, you hear the faint trickle of a little brook or stream. As you make your way toward it, you see it is a narrow brook that flows through grasses and wildflowers. Begin to walk upstream, following the water as it winds around flowers and grasses. The forest that was once in the distance is growing near and you can see the trees that grow around the water, which is flowing more strongly now. Continue to follow the flowing water into the forest and around trees, stones, and a wild creature or two. After what seems like some time, you realize you are deep in the forest and that it has become dark. The trees tower over you and are so thick that they cover the sun. You have become lost.

Up ahead, in the center of the forest, you see flickering lights around a stone basin. As you come closer, you see that there is a small fountain of water bubbling up within the flickering circle of light with a well shaft below. You look around, examining the area, and see little clay figurines, coins, and bits of rags tied on trees. As you gaze back at the water, you see that it has become still. In it, you see the reflection of the moon. But you know that, if you look up, you will see only trees.

As you gaze at the glassy water reflecting the moon, a beautiful woman suddenly begins to take shape under its surface. You lock eyes with her and then you see a thin pale finger emerge from the water. Then a hand. Then her whole arm, clothed in ghostly white with skin so pale it looks almost blue. She emerges from the water from her waist up and tells you to join her there. She takes your hand and you climb in; you begin to sink down slowly into the shaft of the well. It is dark, but her skin glows a faint pale blue/white color. You see images passing by and the sky above you.

Soon, the water becomes a light blue and then a crystal clear white, as you emerge into a silver-colored stone basin surrounded by plants and flowers you have never seen before—all manner of creatures and plants that seem to have faces, and trees that gently wink as you gaze at them. The moon shines high above, lighting the area more than it does in your own realm. As you rest your arms on the stone, you see intricate and unique carvings

Sacred Well Witches

you have never seen before. You climb out of the basin into an enchanted forest and into the realm of the faery.

Take a look around and connect with this realm. When you are ready, travel back the way you came, first by going through the portal of the silver-colored basin, allowing yourself to sink deep down. Then begin reaching up toward the other end of the well shaft, toward the towering trees. When you arrive at the surface, crawl out and retrace your steps. Follow the flowing water out of the forest and back to the meadow with the bright shining sun. Gaze up at the solar energies and return to this world.

Caution: Never eat any food you may be offered! The faery realm can be tricky and its rules and customs can seem foreign. Faeries can be manipulative. It's always best not to take anything from them until you have established a relationship with them. It would be unwise to ignore hundreds of years of folklore that cautions us not to eat the fair folk's food lest we be trapped in their realm. Thanking them can also be taboo, so take care with your choice of words. As with all exercises in this book, feel free to make modifications to suit your environment, your limitations, and the water link you are working with.

Chapter 4

Lake Witches

Lakes, lochs, ponds, and pools are bodies of water surrounded by land that can be either fresh or brackish. Some are manmade, others natural, and some are actually springs. In some cases, they have an underground source; in other cases, they are filled with rain water or seasonal runoff. Wales, Scotland, and England are full of tales of ghosts, witches, magic, and monsters that inhabit these calm bodies of water. To keep things simple here, I will use the word "lake" to mean any one of these water bodies and will only use a specific term for each type when it is necessary to differentiate them.

Lake water is calm and soothing; it can be used for a variety of purposes. Floral essence from flowers that grow by lakes can be used in healing magic, for instance. If you visit a lake on a stormy or cloudy day, you can use the water to work weather magic or to heal your internal storms. Lake water can be used to exorcise baneful enchantments, illness, and spirits. The possibilities are endless. The most important thing to remember about lake water is that it can be used for many things, especially sympathetic magic; like attracts like!

Practitioners traditionally circumambulated a lake three times before entering it to bathe for healing reasons. Offerings, frequently of bread or cloth, were left on the shore or in the water. Coins and other gifts were given to the lake spirit or genius loci. In Dumfriesshire, near Drumlanrig, healers approached a loch called Dhu Loch, or Black Loch, and threw a piece of clothing over their left shoulders into the loch, then carefully gathered water from it without letting it come in contact with the ground. They then turned around sunwise and went home without looking back, as that would break the charm.

LOCHS

Lochs are home to many watery spirits—most famously Lake Ladies, water maidens, water horses, and water bulls or faery cows. In times past, almost every loch had a type of water horse or other spirit that haunted it, sometimes more than one. Loch waters were used to break enchantments and for binding; they were also used as mirrors, and are used today in reflection magic. They are portals to the realm of Annwn and subterranean gardens, and home to the Gwragedd Annwn, the wives of the Underworld who belong to the Welsh fae called Plant Annwn, as well as many other mysterious creatures, including the famous Nessie.

The most famous lochs are found in the UK, and many of them are shrouded in the mists of mystery and folklore, including the Arthurian legend. Here are a few, along with the tales associated them:

- *Llyn Barfog* is home to two different magical tales. One involves King Arthur and a water monster called Afanc; the other includes a white faery cow. It was also said to be home to a group of Gwragedd Annwn, which you will learn about in detail below.

- *Loch Rannoch* is a body of water steeped in mystery. It is said that witches lurked there to harrass the English as they attempted to invade Scotland. Schiehallion Hill, a Caledonian faery hill, is the reputed home of an evil dog who appears from the shadows and follows those who approach the loch's banks. There have also been reports of a white horse that gallops out of the loch and across the moor.

- *Loch ma Naire* was believed to contain waters that had healing value. Folklore tells us that if you entered its waters on the first Monday in August, they held curative properties and could help treat ailments.

- *Dozmary Pool* is said to be the pool where Sir Bedivere returned the famous sword Excalibur to the Lady of the Lake. When King Arthur was mortally wounded, Bedivere, charged with returning the sword, flung it across the lake. The hand of a beautiful mermaid reached up and grabbed it, returning it to its watery depths.

- *Loch Sianta* is located in the north end of Skye. Various offerings were made there and it was said to have curative properties. The loch is actually a spring that looks like a lake, so it is called Loch Sianta.

- *Loch Maree* is located in the highlands and has an island in the middle of it. On this island is a well that was believed to have curative properties. Coins were left in a nearby tree as offerings, and the water was said to cure madness. The cure was procured by first securing a rope made of horse hair under both arms of the one seeking a cure. The person was then tied to a boat and towed around the island several times. To complete the charm, he or she was then taken to the well, dipped into it, and made to drink of its water.

WATER HORSES

The term "water horse" is used to describe beings that are half horse, goat, or bull, and half sea creature. Water horses represent a wide variety of mystical creatures from the Otherworld and the faery world, some of whom are shapeshifters able to change into handsome young men. There are many accounts of water horses from all over the world. Sometimes these creatures are referred to as kelpies or water bulls, but also go by the names hippocampus, aughisky, nuggle, shoopiltee, nojgel, tangi, Cabbyl-Ushtey, Ceffyl dwr, Capall Each-Uisge, Glashtin, Enbarr (Aonbarr or Aenbharr), Each-Uisge, Wihwin, or Nickur.

Water horses can be classified into three categories: helpful, mischievous, and straight-up dangerous. Some are known to help humans and are benevolent—for instance, the hippocampus, water bulls (Tarbh Uisge), faery cows, and Manannán mac Lir's horse, Enbarr (Aonbarr or Aenbharr). Others are completely benign as long as you don't try to ride them, and are sometimes very mischievous. Still others—like kelpies, Aughisky, Cabyll-Ushtey, and Tarroo-Ushtey—are incredibly dangerous and have even been known to eat humans, horses, and other animals. Kelpies have even been described as aquatic demons who cause mischief, drown men, and sink ships.

Water horses have been reported in numerous lochs, including Loch nan Dubhrachan in Skye, Loch Treig (known for being the home of demon horses), North Esk Pool in Agnus, Loch Slochd, Loch Awe, and Loch Rannoch. It was an old Scottish belief that kelpies and water horses could only be killed with silver. They often traveled from loch to loch, mingling with horses at nearby farms. They look just like every other horse, but are dangerous to touch. Those foolish enough to try were often whisked off to the loch as the creature's latest victim.

Kelpies are usually described as young horses, either black or white. Their many names depend on the region in which they lived and the folk stories told of them. They were known to smack the water three times with their tails, which sounded like thunder, then disappear into the water in a flash of lightning. They were also reported in some cases to have magic bridles and were known to cast enchantments on their victims by looking through the holes in the bit of the bridle. Witches or wise women could reverse these enchantments by looking through the bridle backward. It was very rare, but good luck, to possess a kelpie bridle. In Scotland, in one account, a church was built over a pond or loch that was said to have a kelpie living in it. The builders covered the water with iron bars to keep the kelpie in. This reflected the belief that kelpies belonged to the faery realm, as iron was used in many folktales to protect against the faery and to drive them out or trap them.

Water horses appear in folktales around the world. Here are just a few of those legends.

- *The Farmer and the Water Horse*: One day, a farmer saw a strange horse among his farm horses. He tried to drive it away, but it stayed all winter. In the spring, he rounded up his horses, the strange horse included, and prepared to work in the fields, placing a cow shackle around the neck of the strange horse for added security. All summer, the horse worked, leading a team of several horses harnassed together, with the farmer at the front. They worked all summer bringing peat in from the moor. One day, on the way home, when the strange horse became restless and unmanageable, the farmer noticed that his shackle had fallen off. The horse turned to the loch and ran toward it at full speed, with the rest of the horses, who were still harnassed together, trailing behind. The farmer jumped from his mount and managed to cut a few of his horses loose before they went straight into the loch with the water horse. The next morning, the livers of the farmer's horses washed ashore.

- *The Talking Horse at Cru-Loch:* One late night, a man on his way home happened upon a little lake above Ardachyle. By the lake, he saw a horse saddled and ready to ride. As he approached, he saw green water herbs clinging to its feet and ankles. Assuming it was a water horse, he wished the creature well and walked on. As he trudged along, a man (the kelpie now in human form) approached him and told him that, if he hadn't been a friend and wished him well, he would have taken him deep into the loch. The kelpie also told the man the day on which he would die.

Lake Witches

- *Macgregor and the Kelpie Bridle:* A man named Macgregor, traveling from Inverness to Glenlivet, came to rest by Loch Slochd. As he rested, he wished he had a horse to carry him. Suddenly, a horse with a bridle and saddle appeared before him. He mounted the horse and, no sooner than he did, the horse galloped off down the path toward the loch. Macgregor realized that he must have mounted a kelpie. He invoked the Trinity and the horse threw him off, just before diving into the loch. When Macgregor came to his senses, he found the kelpie's magical bridle in his hand. For many years thereafter, he and his descendants worked benevolent magic with this bridle.

- *The Water Horse and the Woman:* A woman who was herding her cattle set them to graze on a hill not far from a lake. Not long after, a young man approached her, laid down, and put his head in her lap. As he stretched out, she saw that he had horse hooves rather than feet. (In one version of this story, she sees that he has water weeds and sand in his hair.) She gently lulled him to sleep, then placed his head on the ground. His head was still on her clothes, however, so she gently cut away her dress, leaving a portion under his head. Then she fled. When the young man woke, he gave a dreadful cry, but the woman had already made her escape!

- *Cumba an Eachuisge—The Lament of the Kelpie:* Kelpies can take human form, as in this story from the Isle of Skye. A kelpie took human form and married a girl named Morag. They lived happily and had a child together. One day, Morag discovered that her husband was not human, so she planned her escape and ran away, breaking the kelpie's heart. Some say they can still hear him singing lullabies to his child in hopes that Morag will return.

- *Nessie:* Many people have heard of the famous monster that lives in Loch Ness, a body of water steeped in mystery and surrounded by ritual burial grounds. Several witches have cast spells on the loch, some to reveal Nessie, others to protect her from monster hunters. Nessie can be worked with as an animal ancestor and, because of her ability to elude the camera and fishermen, the loch itself can be used in sympathetic magic to hide, protect, and travel to watery depths.

LAKE LADIES AND WATER MAIDENS

Lakes, lochs, ponds, and pools have all been known to be the home of water spirits of various kinds. Legends of these creatures abound in Celtic regions, and around the world as well. Mermaids are, no doubt, the best-known water spirits these days, but other water spirits, like the mostly tailless water maidens and Lake Ladies, are just as powerful and dynamic. Mermaids have been spotted living in lakes and lochs, as well as in ponds and pools. In fact, there are many stories of merfolk inhabiting bodies of fresh water of all types—some spring-fed, some not (see chapter 8).

Merfolk are usually described as having mer tails, while Lake Ladies are not—with notable exceptions, like that of Melusine (see chapter 3). These stories—some old and some new—are important to our understanding of the large variety of spirits that dwell in water. As you will see from the stories below, many of these creatures are benevolent, while others are more malevolent. In the case of mermaids and Lake Ladies, these spirits are often described as seductive. As you will see in some of the stories below, they are sometimes very interested in treasure and plants, and in collecting the souls of men.

Childs Ercall Pool

This legend recounts how an old sea captain captured a mermaid and brought her to live at the pool at Childs Ercall. He treated her well, but upon his death, the mermaid was so angry about the way his family had treated him that she swam to the bottom of the pool never to surface again. It is said that she guards a treasure that the captain had found there. On some summer evenings, some say you can hear her sing.

Another tale tells of two men who were walking to work one morning when they passed by Childs Ercall

Pool and saw a mermaid. At first, they were afraid, but she spoke to them with a sweet voice and they instantly fell in love with her. The mermaid told them of a treasure she guarded at the bottom of the pool and swam down to retrieve a piece of it to show them. She surfaced with a very large piece of gold and told them they could have the entire treasure if they would follow her into the pool. So the men waded into the pool up to their chests. When one of the men exclaimed how lucky they were, the mermaid screamed and dove beneath the water, taking the gold with her.

The Witch of Lok Island

This story from Brittany tells of a young man named Houarn and his sweetheart, a young maiden named Bella, who lived in the village of Lannilis. They complained to each other every day about how poor they were, until one day, Houarn became very impatient and told Bella that he was going out into the world to seek their fortune.

Bella took Houarn to her linen press. Removing a little bell, a knife, and a stick from a box, she told him that these relics had been in her family for generations, and that they had magical properties. The bell made a fearsome sound that could be heard at any distance and could warn of danger. The knife could break enchantments and help a person escape the clutches of a witch. The stick, which was more like a staff, could help locate those who were lost. Bella gave Houarn the bell and the knife, but she kept the staff so that she could locate him whenever she wished.

Houarn set off toward the mountains. On his journey, he met two salt merchants who told him how to find the Witch of Lok Island on a small island in a mountain lake on a peak called Hart's Leap Rock. When he arrived at the lake, he found its shores were covered in local plants with beautiful blossoms. He looked around and saw a little boat shaped like a sleeping swan floating in the still waters of the lake, partially hidden in a clump of flowering broom. As Houarn stepped into the boat, the swan woke up and began to swim away from the shore. Soon, it plunged into the water and carried Houarn down to the witch's home in the lake's depths. The witch lived in a beautiful palace made of shells, with a crystal stairway that led up to the door. There were gardens all around where seaweed, diamonds, and flowers mingled to create a beautiful bower that was surrounded by a forest of trees.

Houarn came to the doorway of the palace and saw the witch lying still on a golden bed. She was dressed in fine, soft silk the color of a sea-green wave. Her hair was black, long to the floor, and filled with beautiful coral ornaments. At the sight of her, Houarn stepped back. But the faery woman saw him, rose up, and walked toward him, swaying like the sea. The witch asked him who he was, where he came from, and what he wanted. He answered that his name was Houarn, that he came from Lannilis, and that he was looking for money to buy a cow and a pig.

Pleased with his answer, the witch took him to a room hung with pearls and filled with treasure. She gave him eight golden goblets filled with eight different kinds of wine, which he drank and found to be pleasing. He remembered Bella for a moment, but the wine began to cloud his memory.

The witch then invited Houarn to dine with her and began to prepare a feast, kneeling down and calling fish to her net. One by one, the fish jumped into her net. She placed them in a golden frying pan while whispering softly. Houarn, who could hear the whispers, began to get his wits about him again and felt a wave of regret for having forgotten Bella. Then he became afraid.

The witch served up the fish on a golden dish and Houarn took out the knife Bella had given him. As soon as the knife touched the golden plate, the fish turned into little men who shouted at Houarn that, if he wanted to save himself, he would have to save them. They told him that they too had come to Lok Island seeking their fortunes, but had been ensnared by the witch. They warned him that he too would become a fish in the witch's pond and ultimately be served up as dinner for a newcomer.

Houarn jumped up and rushed to the door, hoping to escape the witch. But she had heard everything. Before he could reach the door, she threw a steel net over him and he turned into a frog. The witch then threw him into the pond with the other enchanted men. As she did so, the bell around Houarn's neck rang out, alerting Bella that he was in danger. Back in Lannilis, Bella quickly dressed and donned her silver cross. Grabbing the magical staff, she set out to find Houarn.

The staff transformed into a chestnut-colored steed, complete with saddle and bridle. Bella mounted the steed and off they went, traveling so quickly that the landscape became a blur. Soon, they reached the foot of the mountain, but it was too high and rocky for the horse to climb. So Bella intoned a brief incantation and the horse grew wings and carried her to the summit. There, she found a nest made of clay and dried moss in which sat a little hobgoblin who shouted with excitement when he saw Bella. Surprised, Bella asked him who he was. He replied that he was Jennick, the husband of the Witch of Lok Island, who had enchanted him. He warned her that Houarn had also fallen under the witch's spell, and told her how to find the island. There, she was to disguise herself as a young man and somehow manage to take the steel net from the witch's belt and trap her in it.

Bella remounted the horse-turned-bird and flew to Lok Island. Once there, the bird transformed back into her staff and she disguised herself, as instructed. She then stepped into the swan boat and was taken to the witch's palace. When the witch saw her, she was delighted, thinking she had trapped yet another handsome young man in her net. As the witch showed Bella the grounds of the palace, she came across Houarn's magical knife, which she tucked away. Following her usual plan, the witch asked Bella if she would stay to dine. Bella, knowing of her enchantments, accepted the invitation, then offered to catch the fish for dinner using the witch's net. The witch gave Bella her net, which Bella threw over her, saying: "May you become what you are in your heart." Immediately, the witch was turned into the Queen of the Toadstools.

Bella removed the enchantments from all the fish in the pond with her magical knife. As she went about this, she noticed a large green frog with a little bell around its neck. Recognizing him as Houarn, Bella touched the frog with the magic knife and he turned back into Houarn.

When Bella was finished removing the enchantments, the hobgoblin arrived and led the lovers to the witch's treasure chest, telling them to take whatever they wanted. Bella ordered the staff to become a wagon to hold the treasure, as well as all the people she had set free. Together, they headed back to Lannilis, where they bought all the land in the parish and settled down with the men they had rescued from Lok Island.

Cerridwen

Cerridwen, who is considered both a Lake Lady and a witch, is first mentioned in *The Black Book of Carmarthen*, but is best known for the part she plays in the story of her cauldron of transformation. Cerridwen, whom many consider to be a goddess, was named in *Ystoria Gwion Bach* as a witch who lived by Llyn Tegid in Penllyn with her two children—a beautiful daughter named Creirwy and an ugly son named Afagddu. After deciding to brew a potion in her cauldron to obtain three drops of Awen (divine inspiration) for her son, she hired a boy named Gwion Bach to tend the cauldron for a year and a day. One day, while he was stirring the cauldron, the boy splashed three drops of the potion onto his thumb. Because it was so hot, he immediately stuck his thumb into his mouth to suck the drops off, and thus became enlightened.

Cerridwen, knowing that only three drops of the potion could be used to bring enlightenment while the rest became poison, grew very angry with the boy. He saw her coming, however, and changed himself into a hare to escape her. In turn, Cerridwen turned into a greyhound and chased the boy toward the river. He dove in and became a salmon; she followed and he became an otter. Cerridwen pursued the boy in the water until he transformed into a bird and fled into the air, where she continued the chase as a hawk, giving him no rest.

Fearing death, the boy saw a heap of winnowed wheat on a barn floor. He changed himself into a grain of wheat and fell into the heap. Cerridwen, still angry, changed herself into a high-crested black hen and began to eat the wheat, eventually swallowing the boy. She carried him for nine months, finally delivering him up to the sea in a leather bag the day before Beltane. In another version of the story, this happens on Samhain. The next day, a young boy named Elphin found the bag and opened it. Seeing a boy's head, he exclaimed: "Behold a Radiant Brow" and thus Taliesin, the Welsh bard, was born.

Gwragedd Annwn

The Gwragedd Annwn (literally, "wives of the Underworld") are faery folk and lake maidens who dwell in the subaqueous realms. They are usually described as tall and thin, with long golden hair. They often took mortal husbands, as in the story of the Lady of Llyn y Fan Fach given below.

In Welsh mythology, Annwn—as well as Annwyn, Annwfn, and other variations—is a name for the Underworld, or what some might call Hell. I call this region the Otherworld. It is important to note, however, that the Celts did not believe in a "hell," in our Western sense. Rather they believed that the spirits of the dead went to a beautiful place called the Summerland. Gwyn ap Nudd, the king of this realm, is often seen leading the Wild Hunt with his Cwn Annwn (Hell Hounds), large white hounds with red-tipped ears. The beings who inhabit the Summerland are called Plant Annwn. The Gwragedd Annwn belong to this group and are found living in the bottoms of lakes in great castles, where they tend beautiful gardens.

Lake Witches

The Gwragedd Annwn are described as tall women robed in blue, green, or white, depending on the story. They are sometimes seen at dusk with Cwn Annwn, and are also often seen with milk-white cows (in other versions, spotted cows) that are said to produce large quantities of milk. One story tells of a farmer who acquired one of these magical cows, which brought him great fortune. After many years, he decided that the cow was old and that it should be brought to market. When the butcher attempted to slaughter the animal, however, the faery cow gave a loud ear-piercing shriek and knocked over nine men. Then the cow heard a loud voice and, when she looked up, she saw Gwragedd Annwn standing high on a cliff above the loch. She called out for the cow to come home to the lake, bringing all her calves up to the fourth generation. Only one cow remained, which turned from white to black. Thus the Welsh cow was born. The farmer was distraught and drowned himself in the lake.

The realm of the Gwragedd Annwn can only be accessed by humans through an opening in a rock close to the lakes in which they dwell. These spirits can also live in rivers, but prefer lonely lakes on mountaintops. Folktales tell of great towers seen under these lakes, and of faery bells that sound in the towers. It was said that, on New Year's Day, the gates to their realm opened, revealing a huge hole in the side of a stone wall or cave. Those who entered found themselves on an island in a lake with beautiful gardens and trees. They were warned not to take anything from this realm into the human world. One fateful day, however, a man decided to take a single flower for luck. Since that day, the gates have never opened.

The Gwragedd Annwn are associated with Llyn Barfog, Lake Crymlyn, and Llyn y Fan Fach. They also are connected to faery cows, or water bulls, a type of benevolent and gentle cow that lives in the lake with the Ladies.

The Lady of Llyn y Fan Fach

This story comes from Myddfai, in South Wales. It is first found in the *Red Book of Hergest* and later in the *Mabinogi*. There are many versions of this legend, although Llyn y Fan Fach is the most famous lake associated with it. Llyn y Forwyn and Llyn Nelferch (Damsels' Pool in Ystrad Tyfodw parish) is also sometimes associated with the story, and locals in these areas sometimes refer to the spirit as Nelferch. Some say that Nelferch is a variation of Alfach or Elfarch. In most versions, the lady of the legend is said to make an appearance around the first of August (The First Harvest, Lammas, Lughnasadh).

One day, a young boy was watching his cows graze in the hills by a lake. A beautiful woman appeared from the lake and he instantly fell in love. He shared some of his bread with her, but she told him it was too hard and disappeared under the water. The next day, the young man brought some soft unbaked bread with him. The lady reappeared and he offered her the loaf. This time, she said it was too soft and sank below the surface again. The following day, the boy brought bread that had been left floating in water. (In another version, he baked her the perfect loaf, neither too hard nor too soft.) When the lady appeared, he offered her the bread and she was very pleased with it. She agreed to marry him on one condition—that he never lay hands on her more than three times in anger. Then she told him to come back the next day.

When the boy returned the next day, a man covered in water plants came to the surface and told him he could marry his daughter if he could pick her out from two identical twins. The boy pondered for a long time, until one of the ladies pushed her foot forward; he saw the gesture and chose correctly. The two were married and the bride brought with her a large dowry of cows. They lived happily and had three sons together.

One day, on the way to town, the wife complained that it was too far to walk. Her husband told her to get the horses and she said she would, as long as he would bring her her gloves. When he returned to find that she had not yet left to fetch the horses, he tapped her on the shoulder with the gloves and said: "Go, go!" She said: "That is the first time you have struck me!" After a time, they went to a wedding and the wife suddenly began to sob. Her husband tapped her on the shoulder and rebuked her for crying. She replied: "I can see this will end in heartbreak. That is the second time you have struck me!" The husband was very careful from then on not to tap his wife in any way.

Then one day, when they were at a funeral, the wife began to laugh. Her husband forgot and tapped her harshly, asking her why she was laughing. She replied: "I rejoice that the person who has died is now happy and no longer suffering. But that is the third and last time you will ever strike me." With that, she called all the animals she had brought with her as a dowry and they all sank under the waters of the lake, including one recently slaughtered cow who jumped off its hook and joined them. It is said that the wife emerged from the lake several times to visit her three sons, and that she gave them the gift of healing and a knowledge of herbs. They eventually became the famous physicians called the Meddygon of Myddfai, whose family line can be traced to the mid 1800s.

The Lady of the Lake

The most famous story about a Lake Lady comes from old Arthurian tales. There are many different versions of this legend and much controversy over which are true. The Lady of the Lake in these tales is also called Nimue, Argante Viviane, Elaine, Ninianne, Nineveh, Evienne, or Nivian. Though the stories vary, it is widely believed that the term "Lady of the Lake" was a title, not a name, and that Morgan Le Fay may have held this title. It may even be that "Morgan" itself was a title.

The name Morgan means "sea born," which alludes to her being born of the sea or water. This leads us to the possibility that she, in fact, was a spirit of the faery realm. Indeed, many believe her to be one of the Welsh and Breton water spirits called Mari-Morgans, who, like the Gwragedd Annwn, were believed to live in castles and villages under lakes. Usually found in groups of nine, these beautiful women were often seen combing their hair and luring sailors to a watery death.

According to medieval literature, Morgan was trained in the ways of magic by Merlin, a wizard and wild man. In one story, after she has learned magic from him, Morgan traps Merlin beneath a root (or in a stone, or in a cave, or in the trunk of a tree, depending on the telling) and later carries the mortally wounded Arthur to Avalon. It was only after the 11th century, when Lancelot appeared in the tales, that the sword Excalibur was added to the narrative. In these later versions, she enchants the sword and bestows it on King Arthur. In the legend recorded by Sir Thomas Malory, she is named Nimue and portrayed as one of the three women dressed in black who ferried Arthur's body to Avalon on a barge navigated by Barinthus, the Avalonian version of Charon, the boat man who navigates the River Styx.

Avalon itself is strongly connected to the Arthurian legends. King Arthur was conceived at Tintagle Castle, which is a coastal castle near Saint Michaels Mount, while the putative graves of Arthur and Guinevere were found at Glastonbury. Lundy, which is featured in the *Mabanogi*, is also associated with King Arthur and his knights. It is not surprising, therefore, that we can trace the origins of the Lady of the Lake, one of the most important female characters in Arthurian lore, to this place.

What many don't understand, however, is how important Morgan is, and that her role is much deeper than portrayed in the modern Arthurian tales produced by Hollywood. She is, in fact, one of the sisters of Avalon—a demi-goddess and water fae, and also quite possibly a Gwragged Annwn. Some even identify her as one of the nine sisters who appear in many folktales as healers or priestesses who are able to manipulate the elements and control events through their powers of witchcraft. Another group of nine women, known as the Korrigan, were beautiful faery beings with red eyes who changed into hags every morning. These sisters were depicted as sorceresses and shapeshifters, and as sirens who lured men to watery graves. Geoffrey of Monmouth, in *The Vita Merlini*, claims that Morgan Le Fay was the chief of nine sisters. Other texts portray her as a priestess of Avalon, as a healer, and as a cousin, sister, or enemy of King Arthur. Though many of these texts demonize her, Morgan is, in fact, first and foremost a faery woman, a demi-goddess, and a healer. She was a great necromancer who had the power to part the veil between worlds, and some say that she ruled the Underworld.

THE CAILLEACH AND OTHER WATER SPIRITS

The cailleach is a giantess associated with winter who is believed to have formed Loch Awe, or at the very least, is associated with it. She is also connected with Loch Eck. She roams the land with her goats. Each morning, she removes capstones from wells and lets the waters flow; each evening, she returns the caps so the water doesn't flood the land. In one story, the giantess falls asleep by a well and fails to cap it, causing everyone in the nearby village to drown. Legend has it that this is how Loch Awe was formed. Another story has her forming Loch Ness in a fit of anger. In a different version of this story, the cailleach hires a young maiden named Nessa to uncap one of the two wells in Inverness and recap it at night. One day, Nessa arrives late to cap the well and finds its waters flowing toward her. In her fear, she runs. Seeing this from Ben Nevis, the cailleach cursed Nessa to run forever, thus creating the River Ness and Loch Ness. Once a year, Nessa emerges from the loch and sings her beautiful lament.

Cailleach are found in a number of traditions and legends. Here are a few that give you a taste of how they fit into the folklore of different regions.

- *Cailleach Bheur* is associated with the Corryvreckan whirlpool on the Isle of Jura. The name of this whirlpool means "cauldron of plaid," because it was believed that the cailleach washed her plaid clothing in its waters. When the plaid had been washed until it turned white, winter was upon the land. Sailors used this pool for weather divination as well. In other areas of Scotland, this spirit was associated with storms, tides, and shipwrecks.

- *Cailleach Uisg* means water cailleach, which connects her with Nicnevin and with water nymphs. She is also connected with winter and is often thought of as the crone of winter, when frozen water in the form of ice and snow covers the earth with a soft white blanket.

- *The Heron of Loch a-na-cailleach* is the name of a cailleach who once lived in the woods near a loch. Her presence was said to spread disease among the local people and animals. The only person who was immune to her influence was the local minister, whose prayers thwarted her magic, annoying her mightily. The local folk finally begged him to drive her out and he did so using holy water. Unfortunately, she simply took up residence in the local standing stones near the loch, where the villagers saw her by moonlight flying in the form of a heron. They tried their best to shoot her down, but never succeeded. A retired highland sergeant once hunted her all through the night, only to see her rise from the mist in the morning. He went after her with a gun loaded with silver buttons and a crooked sixpence. He was discovered later that day unconscious, battered, and with his gun exploded. But by his side lay a great blue heron—dead. The cailleach's ghost allegedly still haunts the loch.

- *Gwrach y Rhibyn* is a hag of the mist, a spirit that lives in dripping fog, appearing in the shape of a hag or shriveled old woman. Like the banshee, her shriek foretells misfortune or death.

Chapter 5

🐚

Marsh Witches

Marshes, swamps, bogs, and wetlands are all types of low, uncultivated terrain where water tends to collect and that is dominated by trees. Wetlands are areas of low land where plants, trees, and grasses grow. Marshes often only support the growth of reeds and tall grasses, while bogs have poor nutrients and support mostly peat. Water in these areas is often only a few feet deep, and in some seasons or during drought may dry up altogether. Marshes are generally dominated by herbaceous plants rather than trees, as are peat bogs and salt marshes. Of all the bodies of water covered in these chapters, none is more dark, mysterious, and full of peril than these shallow watery places.

Witches who work in this environment find value in the medicine of shed snake skins, bones, and eggs, as well as all manner of teeth, spiders, and feathers. The water with which they connect and from which they draw their powers is dark and murky green, and filled with lurking serpents and poisonous creatures. To keep things simple here, I will refer to the witches who inhabit all these types of terrain as marsh witches. Although there is limited documented folklore about marshes and marsh witches, the archetypal image of these witches comes easily to mind when we think about them and read their stories.

Marshes and bogs have always been considered places of curses, dark magic, ghosts, monsters, and even sacrifice. This is only one side of the story, however. There is a lighter side to these watery places that is often ignored. Marshes are dark and full of death, but they are also places that are full of light and life. They hold the energy of yin and yang, of light and dark, of death and rebirth. They are an important part of our ecosystem because they are home to hundreds of animals, birds, reptiles, and plants, and they are calm and peaceful places where healing can take place. The magic of these places reminds us that we need to get our hands wet and our feet deep in the muck to access the spirits that live there.

Marshes and bogs have always been thought of as magical. They were considered sacred places by our Celtic ancestors. In 1950, archeologists uncovered the Tollund Man, the naturally mummified corpse of a man who lived during the 4th century BC in Scandinavia. On examination, this "bog body" provided striking evidence that sacrifices had once been performed in the surrounding bogs—perhaps of kings or royal figures. Evidence has also been found that cattle were similarly sacrificed to the gods in these locations. To date, over 1800 bodies have been found, although many were lost in WWII and others fell apart or were not properly preserved.

Witchcraft is about duality and balance; accepting the dark is just as important as seeking the light. Yet all the marsh witches I have ever known or read about will place a curse on you in a hot minute if they feel so inclined. They truly are witches of murky magic. Considering the thick death energy that hangs over bogs and marshes, it is not surprising that the shadowy witches who work there employ bones, animal carcasses, and poisons in their craft. In fact, the tools used by marsh witches vary markedly from those used by sea, lake, or well witches. A working marsh witch uses tools like bone, spider webs, toads, teeth or claws, marsh grasses and reeds, and perhaps even albino buck skins or horn sheds. They use baskets, knives, jars, and gloves—but you probably won't find them creating spells with crystals or store-bought herbs.

Animal allies for marsh witches include snakes, toads, frogs, and spiders. Serpents of all kinds are great allies for them as well—both poisonous and nonpoisonous—and small rodents and birds of all kinds are closely allied to them. Spiders have a close connection to marsh witches, as they are both destroyers and creators. Other allies include otters, beavers, heron, rabbits, butterflies, shrimp or crawdad, dragonflies, muskrats, ducks, bats, and kingfishers. When working in marshes and bogs, however, always be cautious and do not put yourself in danger by approaching the wildlife found there.

Folktales abound that tell of witches who work in marshes and bogs. Here are just a few to give you a feeling for the power of marsh magic:

- *Yr Hen Wrach (The Old Witch):* East of Aberystwyth lived an old Gwrach y Rhibyn, or marsh witch, who had a habit of luring men to their deaths in the nearby bogs and marshes. Local folk told how, on autumn evenings, she walked through the village opening doors and breathing on the people who resided there, giving them a nasty fever. The villagers didn't understand why she was so grumpy toward them, but eventually they came to the conclusion that she was angry because they were cutting peat too close to her home. They moved their efforts to the other side of the bog and, soon after, the trouble stopped. The villagers later reported seeing the witch in the dark and liminal hours floating along a few feet above the ground with her cape flapping behind her.

- *The Laidly Worm of Spindleston Heugh:* A king and queen once lived in Bamburgh Castle with their two children, Margaret and Childe Wind. One day, the queen died and the king wished to remarry. While hunting in the woods, he came upon a woman and, not knowing she was a witch queen, he married her. When he did, his daughter was enchanted and transformed into a worm. The king consulted a wizard, who told him that Margaret's brother must give her three kisses to restore her to her maidenly form. The king, finding the witch queen near a well by the keep, took three drops of water from the well and flung it at her, turning her into a wrinkled frog. In an alternative version, the witch queen is struck with a rowan-wood wand.

- *Aunt Alsey:* Aunt Alsey was an elderly woman who was believed to have a toad for a soul-animal. One day, she was quarreling with the pregnant wife of a shopkeeper over rent that was owed. Aunt Alsey left the shop in a huff. Shortly thereafter, a toad dropped from the ceiling onto the pregnant woman, who screamed loudly. He husband came running and threw the toad into the fire. They called the doctor and began to prepare for a premature birth, as the toad had greatly upset the wife. The shop-keeper then found that the toad had tried to escape the fire and was badly burned, but not dead. He grabbed it with tongs and threw it back into the fire. Soon after, news came that Aunt Alsey had also fallen into a fire and was now dead.

- *Toad on the Road:* An old Cornish tale tells of a farm-er's wife who was arguing with an old woman she met on the road who had a reputation for being a witch. Eventually, the woman mounted her horse and rode on. After a time, however, the horse had to stop because the road was covered in toads. The more the woman tried to move forward, the more toads appeared in the road. After a while, a carriage approached. When the woman asked for help getting past the toads, the carriage's passengers said that they had been following her for some distance and had seen no sign at all of a single toad.

- *The Harpist of Ysbyty Ifan:* There was once a young harp player who ventured out one day toward Ysbyty Ifan, where he was to play his harp at a wedding. On the way, he fell into a bog. He struggled and struggled, until the bog sucked him down. In one last effort to escape, he threw back his head and emitted a wild scream. Not long after, a bunch of little men appeared and threw him rope. They hauled him out and took him to a house where he was given fine clothes. There, he danced the night away with a beautiful little woman, reveling until the party was over. He awoke to find a dog licking his face. He was lying against a wall, with his clothes and harp covered in bog mud.

MARSH CREATURES

Tales of witchcraft, charms, and spells associated with marsh- and bog-dwelling creatures abound in Celtic lands, and throughout Europe as well. One Cornish tradition suggests that tying a string around the neck of a live toad and hanging it until the body drops off, then tying the same string around your own neck until your fifteenth birthday protected against quinsy, an infection behind the tonsils. Another claims that bones taken from the left side of a green frog that has been eaten by ants will provoke hatred, while bones taken from the right side will excite love. The frog bones were obtained by placing a frog in a container with holes in it, then placing the container on an anthill; the ants removed the flesh and left only the bones. Some believed that bones acquired in this way brought misfortune to anyone who received them.

One charm that was used for luck and prosperity called for placing the bones of a tree frog in a small bag with teeth that had been buried for several years, then rubbing the bag over an item to enchant it. This was especially useful for items people wanted to sell, as it attracted many customers. In France, placing a toad on the left breast of a woman made the person who placed it there privy to her secrets.

Toads and frogs were said to aid in fertility, and many effigies or dried frogs were left as votive offerings at churches by women wanting to conceive. This practice was especially common in Eastern Europe. They were also used for weather magic, rain summoning, transformation, evolution, coming into creative power, cursing, power over others, and witchcraft. As amphibious creatures who journeyed between the worlds of earth and water, frogs and toads were also often used as spirit familiars, guardians, and in birth charms, and were associated with rebirth, transformation, and shapeshifting because of the metamorphosis involved in their own life cycle.

Another common practice called for ground frog bones to be formed into pills or capsules and fed to someone to attract that person as a lover. In Lincolnshire, women ensnared reluctant bridegrooms by participating in communion, but not swallowing the wafer. Instead, they kept it and, when leaving the church, spat it out in front of a toad. If the toad ate it, the man in question would agree to marry the woman performing the spell the next time he saw her. If not, the union was not meant to be. Similar practices were used to determine if some-one should become a witch.

Katherine Thompson and Anne Nevelson were Northumberland cunning women who were convicted in 1604 for placing the bill of a white duck into the mouth of someone they were trying to cure. They were also accused of mumbling charms and working with frogs and spiders, and encouraging people to eat them or place them on body parts that needed healing. In Devonshire, a toad charm used to destroy a witch's power was made by taking three toad hearts and impaling them on or studding them with thorns. These were then placed in three narrow-necked jars with a frog liver suspended on pins. The jars were each taken to a different church yard and buried exactly seven inches underground and exactly seven feet from the church entrance, while the Lord's Prayer was recited backward. Those who performed this rite were believed to be protected from witches' enchant-ments for the rest of their lives. A story from the late

1800s tells of a woman who carried a dried frog in her pocket to protect herself from smallpox. In Hereford-shire, a Romany woman recommended that a man with an abscess on his arm catch a live toad, cut off its leg, and then let the frog go. He wore the leg in a silk bag around his neck for three weeks and was reportedly cured.

Charms like these are found throughout the British Isles. In Yorkshire, one charm used nine toads to gain the power of the evil eye. The toads were strung together as a garland that was then buried, giving the person work-ing the charm the power to inflict harm. It was believed that, as the toads decomposed, sickness or sorrow would grow in the victim. In East Anglia, witches took the spit-tle from a toad and mixed it with sap from a sow thistle to create an invisibility charm. They applied this ointment to their bodies in the shape of a cross. Another charm claimed that carrying a frog heart under the right arm gave the same results. In Hertfordshire, it was believed that a thief who wore a toad's heart around the neck could avoid detection. And in Staffordshire, it was con-sidered very unlucky to throw hair from a comb or brush out the window, lest a toad use it to give you a persistent toothache or headache.

Bullrushes were also used in marsh magic to ambush and curse, and it was considered very unlucky to bring them into the home. Stump water, which is water that has naturally collected in a tree stump, was considered to have healing properties and was used to remove warts, as well as in luck charms. A rabbit's foot dipped in stump water three times was considered lucky. The same water, carried in a vial, was said to give the wearer great power. Because stump water is "silent" or stagnant water, it was believed to possess the ability to communicate with ancestral spirits, especially if the tree it was taken from had ancestral or necromantic properties, because the water retained the power of the tree where it was found. In some places, stump water is considered holy and is used in ritual. In Europe, the water may have a connection with the faery realm, especially if it is found in a hollow tree rather than a stump. Likewise, water pooled in a basin formed by tangled roots has curative properties and was used in hair-growth charms.

In Wales, people burned snake skins and preserved the ashes to use in various charms. Mixing the ash in a salve helped heal wounds. Placing the ash between your shoulder blades made you invulnerable. Mixing it in water and washing your face with it scared all your enemies away. Casting the ash in their home made neighbors leave, while placing it under your feet made everyone agree with you. Putting the ashes under your tongue helped you win a fight, and putting a pinch on your forehead before bed encouraged prophetic dreams. Throwing the ash on someone's clothing made the person speak only the truth. Placing the ash between your hands and washing them, keeping some between them, made everyone love you.

TOADS AND FROGS

Toads and frogs have been associated with witchcraft from as far back as Roman times, and possibly even before. We've already seen how they were used in rites and rituals across a number of cultures going back over the centuries. But the power associated with these creatures is so strong, and the folklore surrounding them is so persistent and so pervasive, that I think they deserve a closer look here.

In eastern England, magicians called toadmen were believed to have psychic powers and to possess power over animals, horses, and women. They obtained their powers through second sight and by retrieving what was known as a "key bone" from a toad used in ritual. Although frogs could be used for this purpose as well, toads were believed to be more powerful. During the Roman occupation, the Romans used toads as compasses by placing knives on their backs, believing that the toad would orient itself in the correct direction.

Frogs and toads are amphibians that, since medieval times, have been closely associated with witchcraft in general and with marsh magic in particular. There are stories aplenty of women shapeshifting into animals— often cats or toads—who were then thought to hold the spirit of the witch. This entity is called a *fetch,* and toads were often used as fetches in witchcraft. The concept of a fetch can be hard to grasp if you are unfamiliar with it. Think of a fetch as a shell waiting to receive the spirit of a witch when it leaves the human body and enters another being or object. By entering a fetch, the spirit of the witch has the freedom to roam over many realms. Likewise, it was believed that, if a witch's fetch were harmed, the witch would be harmed as well.

The tales of toads and frogs being used in charms and spells are legion. Wearing parts of a toad around the neck was said to protect against swelling, tuberculosis, and rheumatism. The ashes of a burned frog or toad worn around the neck protected against the black plague. Sometimes, the back legs of frogs were worn instead, the belief being that, by transference, the disease would pass to the still-living top portion of the frog's body, which would then crawl away, taking the disease with it. Effigies of toads and frogs made from silver, wax, wood, and iron that are believed to have been votive offerings have been found by archaeologists. Toads were associated with love and it was believed that their blood had aphrodisiac properties. Pliny was the first to write that they could be worn as an aphrodisiac amulet. They were also associated with treasure and some, believing that toads guarded treasures, were kind to them in hopes of sharing in the riches.

Toads and frogs were also associated with poison. A particular species of venomous toad, called rubeta, is said to have wonderful powers because it lives among brambles. Certain species of toxic toads were used to poison, or attempt to poison, the enemies of the powerful. Although frogs and toads were considered beneficial and used in healing in pre-Christian rites, they took on a darker, grimmer connotation of fear and disgust in the Christian era in Europe, when they gained a sinister reputation and were associated with the devil or with evil spirits. In France, they were sometimes called *bot*, a name also used for the devil. Because they metamorphosed from tadpole to mature animal, they were also linked to the moon and its phases, and were used in alchemy as an agent of change.

Sometimes, the magical properties attached to toads and frogs were contradictory. In England, it was believed that a toad could cure warts or even cancer by rubbing the toad on the afflicted area. Of course, magical transference was used here. On the other hand, in other places in England and Europe, it was believed that toads caused warts. In Scotland, it was believed lucky for a toad to cross a bride's path on her wedding day, while in Britain, it was thought very unlucky for a toad to cross on your left side. In Scotland, during harvest season, a toad was rubbed on the sprained wrists of field hands to provide relief. They were also thought to help cure thrush, and in some cases were placed in the mouth for a few moments. Today we know that, in this case, it was probably the antifungal properties of the toad that helped cure the condition. I don't recommend trying this, but it is interesting to know the old folk beliefs.

Toad stones, also called bufonite and *bufonis lapis*, were believed to come from the head of a toad but were actually part of a fossilized fish from the Jurassic and Cretaceous periods. The teeth of Lepidotes, an extinct genus of ray-finned fish, look like little round black or brown pebbles. These were highly prized and thought to be rare jewels. This may be what Shakespeare was alluding to in *As You Like It* when he wrote of the ugly toad that yet wears a precious jewel in its head. During the Middle Ages and up to the 18th century, this stone was thought to change color when brought into proximity with poison. The stone was often worn as a ring, and was considered to be as precious as a pearl. People used it as a protective amulet for homes and boats, and believed it would bring victory to those who wore it in a fight. It also protected against lightning, enchantments, and witchcraft, and was prized by pregnant women, who believed it could protect them from evil and help them with women's problems and in childbirth.

In Cornwall, to find a toad in a mine shaft was considered lucky. To find a toad on your path was also lucky, but to frighten him away was considered very unlucky. One "toad doctor" cut the hind legs off toads, placed them in bags, and hung the bags around his patients' necks, letting the legs quiver against their chests. This was considered a remedy for Kings' Evil, a condition of the cervical lymph nodes associated with tuberculosis. This practice persisted up to the mid-1800s. Indeed, frogs have been used in all manner of strange cures, from stopping nose bleeds and heavy menstrual flow, to rubbing them on the bottoms of the feet to treat diseases of the head and heart. They were hung by their back feet in chimneys, dried in the sun, chopped and powdered, and used in spirits, oils, and volatile salts.

Toads were also used in various forms of divination called *batrachomancy*, although not much information on this practice survives. The word itself comes from the Greek word *batrakhos*, meaning "frog," and *manteia*, meaning "prophecy." Some say witches counted the warts on toads to divine the future, while others simply watched the toad and divined the future by its actions. Because toads and frogs are associated with water, they were most often used to predict the weather. Many toads were said to predict the coming of wet weather or rain.

One solitary rite found in many different old texts, with slight variations for specific outcomes or uses, involved using the bones of an impaled toad set upon a river or stream as a rite of initiation into the European Cunning path of witchcraft and the Toad—a path followed by solitary European witches and village healers who used natural remedies, gave advice, foretold the future, and dealt in other forms of magic in their villages. These practitioners, who were often called wise women or conjure men, used old folk charms, magical herbs, and Biblical psalms to enchant and heal.

OTHER MARSHY SPIRITS

Working with the spirits who dwell in marshes and bogs is different from working with those who inhabit rivers, lakes, wells, and oceans. Marshy waters and the spirits that live there often have a darker nature. Of course, that is not always the case, as many benevolent water spirits are found there as well. But in the dark waters of marshes, you may find phantom ghosts, spectral animals like white deer or black dogs, and entities that will lead you into dark watery tree-covered places—perhaps for magic or mischief. In the murky green waters of marshes (especially in Britanny), you may find the Corrigans (sometimes spelled with a "k"), souls in pain who are condemned to wander through wastelands and wetlands. These are sometimes described as small gnome-like creatures, and sometimes as beautiful whispy female forms with white or blond hair and red eyes who, in the morning, turn into hags. These siren-like spirits were often seen haunting founts and waterfalls. Most of the time, however, they are heard and not seen.

You may even come across spirits of the dead, who have been said to roam across lonely marshlands. One such encounter occurred on the road from Carnac, when a traveler saw a woman from Kergoellec whom he knew to be dead for at least eight days. As he approached her, he asked her to move so he could pass and she vanished. The same traveler then saw her at the Marsh of Breno, where he tried to speak with her.

The marsh spirit you are most likely to encounter, however, is Jenny (sometimes Jinny or Ginny) Green Teeth, a spirit strongly associated with duckweed, a green algae found on the surface of still bodies of water and sometimes on the bottoms of trees that grow near water. Jenny is a water spirit from Gothic mythology who is believed to inhabit any pond or still body of water where duckweed is found. She is described as having long fingers and nails, pale green skin, very long hair, large eyes, a pointed chin, and green (sometimes pointed) teeth. But Jenny isn't the only spirit who lives in marshes and bogs. In Cornwall, there are reports of mischievous water spirits who lure passersby into their bog with the light from the lanterns they carry. This atmospheric ghost light, sometimes called Will-o-the-wisp, is seen by travelers at night, especially over bogs, swamps, or marshes. A simple folk remedy to protect against these little water spirits was to turn your clothing or coat inside out.

DEW

Dew is another interesting type of water that has magical properties. It has been used in beauty routines, healing, cursing, and various other enchantments. In Morva, Zennor, and Towednack, dirty or lazy children and women were taken away by the fair folk, carefully cleansed with dew, and then returned. It was thought that, because they were washed by the fair folk in morning dew, they became more beautiful. The Anglo-Saxons and Irish believed that dew was useful in matters concerning the eye, to help improve sight, and to remove eye pain. Dew collected from fennel was believed to help strengthen sight.

Dew was thought to have healing properties if taken from hawthorn or other magical plants. Collected and applied before sunrise on May Day (Beltane, May 1st), Midsummer, or the summer solstice, it was believed to have powers that were increased by the strength of the sun, which was at its height at these times. Dew was also thought to remove freckles and warts, and to help beautify, as described in this old charm:

> The Maiden fair, who on the first day of May
> Ventures to the field at the break of day,
> There she washes her face in dew
>   from the faery hawthorn tree,
> Will forever after extremely beautiful be.

Some believed these healing properties could be transferred by running through dew-soaked grass. One British charm to heal a child with a weak back involved leading the child through dew-soaked grass on three consecutive days starting on May Day. Dew collected from under an oak or hawthorn tree before dawn on May Day helped with the complexion and was used in beauty routines. It was also used to bathe weak and sickly children to increase their strength.

Dew can also be used for protection. Dew gathered on Saint George's day, April 23, was used to protect from the evil eye. On the Isle of Man, bathing the face in dew was believed to protect you from witchcraft for a year. In Britain, dew collected from a graveyard was said to protect against neck swelling. A dew-soaked bone retrieved from a graveyard was rubbed on an inflicted area, then returned to the same place and buried. Through transference, as the bone rotted away, the disease receded from the body.

In England, wise women regarded dew as a gift from heaven and used it as an additive in their medicines. They usually collected it from stones with depressions or cups carved in them called Bullaun Hole. Dew collected with a white rag, or from a white rag placed outside but not touching the ground, was used in rites of healing. Sometimes the dew itself was used; sometimes the rag was used to wrap the afflicted part of the body.

Dew collected to harm others was used in a practice called dew witching. And it was believed that, if witches gathered dew from a field of cattle, they would be harmed. Adding a spoonful of dew to a butter churn was said to produce a good supply.

Exercise: Dark Still Waters Meditation

We've seen in this chapter that bogs and marshes hold darker, decaying, and still energies. If you are lucky to live near one of these areas, or even one that is similar, take the time to meditate with these waters. I suggest doing the meditation at dusk, during the waning moon or Dark Moon. However, if you are particularly drawn to this type of water, consider meditating with the water at different times of the day and during different moon cycles. If you don't live near this type of water, you can still connect with it through remote viewing or visualization.

Locate a body of marshy or still water where it is safe for you to sit for a while and meditate. Once you have settled in, close your eyes and bring yourself into a very light trance or meditative state. Begin to listen. What sounds do you hear? What does the air feel like? What do you smell? After a while, in your mind's eye, stand up and enter the marsh. On the astral plane, sense what the water feels like. How does it compare to the smells and sounds in the mundane world?

You can exit the mediation at this point by drawing back into your body and coming back to the present moment. If you want to continue, begin to speak with the local spirits. Who comes forth? Is it Jenny Green Teeth? An ancestral spirit? A local faery? Since the nature of marsh spirits can be unpredictable, I suggest only making contact at first and speaking with them. Don't interact, accept food or gifts, or follow them to their watery homes. These practices are better left to more advanced spirit workers.

Chapter 6

Sea Witches

Sea witches have delighted the mind of many for hundreds of years; their mythology and folklore are vast. Many tales have been told about sea witches, and many more about ghostly women wandering the shores. Much of the lore we have about sea witches comes from Britain, although there is not much information on specific magical practices related to the sea that comes directly from the Celts. The lore has come to us, instead, in remnants passed on through folktales and folk magic practices.

Sea witches have a long-standing reputation for lurking upon the shores, selling charms, calling up storms, and sinking ships. Some sea witches—especially those from stories collected from the New World and into the 19th century—were reported to wear red shoes. In fact, this was believed to be a sure sign of a witch. The stories that follow have been collected and retold, sometimes as slightly different versions of the same legends that have been woven into one story. Some are quite detailed;

others less so. But each constitutes an important piece of a working practice based on the folklore of sea witchery.

- *Nancy, the Sea Witch of Newlyn:* a witch whose divination tools are found in the Museum of Witchcraft. She cast belemnites and sea stones and read how they fell, making oracular predictions for fishermen.

- *The Witch of Fraddam:* a notorious witch from the West Country who was said to have pledged her soul to the devil. She was said to be in a battle, or witch war, with the Enchanter of Pengerswick, who is described as a white witch who continually thwarted her magic. One day, she went to Kynance Cove to give the Enchanter's horse poison water and to drench him in a poison brew described as hell broth that was brewed from poison ingredients on the blackest of nights during the most evil aspects of the stars with the help of the devil himself. Around the time of the spring equinox, and under a stormy sky, she rode her black ram-cat across the moors. When the Enchanter approached, she prepared to throw her cauldron of hell broth at the horse, but her plan went awry when the horse looked up at her with fire in his eyes. In her fright, she spilled the hell broth and, as the cauldron went over, it hit her on the leg and she tripped and fell in. The cauldron instantly became her coffin. To this day, she can be seen bobbing up and down in the sea in her cauldron, causing all manner of mischief. It is said that the Enchanter alone has power over her and calls her to do his bidding by standing on the shore and blowing his trumpet three times.

- *The Sea Witch of Penryn:* also called Kate "the gull" Turner and Kata de Mar. She is known for her work in divination. In one source, she is described as using a "talking tambourine" along with cowrie shells to perform her divinatory magic. Her tambourine was painted with magical symbols and divided into sections in order to divine the meaning of the message by where the shells fell. She also used sand dollar doves, Aristotle's lanterns, and other shells.

- *The Sea Witch of Mevagissey:* a witch who used the tusks of sperm wales in "stroking magic." She sat and stroked a tusk while chanting a spell—one for benevolent magic, another for baneful magic.

- *The Ship-Sinking Witch of Ireland:* a tale from the folklore of the Emerald Isle. One day, local fishermen were bringing in their catch when they were approached by an old woman who demanded that they give her some of the fish for her meal. They refused, and she warned them they would be sorry. That evening, the fishermen reported seeing her outside her home performing strange rites that involved a bowl of water with several feathers floating on it. As she stirred the water, a storm began to brew out at sea. The next morning, the shore was covered with wrecked ships and the bodies of fishermen. The townsfolk and the families of the lost fishermen blamed the witch, but she was nowhere to be found.

- *The Galligende:* a group of nine Gaulish priestesses who lived on Sena, an island just off the coast of Brittany. They were known to have great magical and oracular powers, and were reputed to be perpetual virgins. (This differentiates them from the Namnetes below.) Their powers were such that they could charm the ocean and stir up fierce storms. They could shapeshift into any animal they wished, and had the power to cure incurable diseases. Many travelers and seafarers went to them for luck, protection, and healing.

- *The Namnetes:* a group of Gallic priestess-like women who lived on a small island at the mouth of the River Loire that was inhabited only by women. No man dared set foot on the island, but the women often left to visit men, to have intercourse with them, and to bear their children. They were said to worship Dionysus and performed sacred and initiatory rites. Once a year, they removed the roof of their temple and replaced it the very same day. If any woman dropped her load during this work, she was set upon by the rest and torn to pieces. Her load was then carried around the temple to shouts of "Ev-ah."

FLOTSAM AND JETSAM

Flotsam and jetsam are more than just words that are fun to say. They are actually concepts regulated by maritime law—a body of law that governs and adjudicates offenses, claims, and events that occur on the sea. In general, the terms "flotsam" and "jetsam" are used to describe two distinct types of debris found in the ocean—most often from shipwrecks or other disasters.

Jetsam derives from the word "jettison." Jetsam is thus debris that has been deliberately thrown overboard. This usually occurs when a ship is in distress and crew members discard cargo to lighten the load. Jetsam is often composed of parts of a ship, or its cargo or equipment that have been purposefully removed. Flotsam derives from the French word *floter,* meaning "to float." Flotsam is thus floating debris from a cargo ship that is shipwrecked. Maritime law makes a clear distinction between flotsam and jetsam, because, while jetsam may be claimed by anyone who discovers it, flotsam can be claimed only by the original owner. Flotsam cannot be sold; jetsam can. And it is often quite valuable.

A venter, on the other hand, is any item or object that has been washed up on the tide or driven ashore by wind. This may include flotsam or other objects from a shipwreck. Because venters, when found, could be claimed, they were often associated with helping ordinary people get rich or with having good fortune. If you have ever spent time combing a beach, you know that all manner of venters wash up there. Lost goods, antiques, and other treasures are often found and collected by beachcombers and clever sea witches alike!

MOON MAGIC

As witches and water magicians, we must learn to understand the moon's cycles. The moon is intimately connected with witchery in general, and with water or sea witches in particular. Our bodies are made up of 70 to 80 percent water. So if the moon affects the tides, it affects us as well. More babies are born during the Full Moon, for instance, and people often act mad during this lunar phase—which is where the term "lunacy" comes from.

Shellfish and other sea creatures spawn and mate during the tidal cycles, which are driven by the moon's gravitational pull. Before clocks, the moon was used to keep time and it is still used in moon magic to time cycles, to start and end workings, and even to determine a monthly ritual schedule. Every month, the moon travels through its cycle of phases. Each cycle is 29.5 days long; this is how we can end up with two Full Moons in some months. This phenomenon, called a blue moon, occurs when the moon becomes full twice in one month.

If you don't already, start to observe the moon's cycles. Begin with the Full Moon and watch the moon each night until it has completed a full cycle. Once the moon has reached its peak fullness, it begins to shrink in size. In a sense, it sheds its skin—each night shaving a little off and keeping it from our sight. This is only an illusion, as it just obscures parts of itself during its cycle, eventually hanging dark in the sky with nothing visible but a shadow. Then we begin to see the moon grow again—first a small sliver, then more and more, until it has returned to its full phase. Of course, we know that the moon itself doesn't actually change. It is our perception that changes. This reminds us of our own shadow work and how even light contains the duality of darkness.

You are most likely already familiar with how the moon's cycles work. From a young age, we are all drawn to the moon and, subconsciously and consciously, watch it wax and wane. But how does this relate to magic? It relates to magic because the moon's cycle interacts with the earth's gravitational pull, which affects our own energies and those of the tides. It is an otherworldly reminder of the female energies of earth, water, and sky, and—if you think about it—fire as well, for we would not see the moon's brilliant face if the sun did not illuminate it for us.

The moon's phases run in regular cycles, and each phase plays a particular role in our magic:

- *Full Moon:* when the moon has reached its fullest phase. This energy is powerful for manifesting, cleansing, and anything else that needs some extra *pow!* Set your stones, crystals, runes, alrunes, herbs, and shells out during this time for cleansing and to charge them under the Full Moon's energy.

- *Waning moon (getting smaller):* when the moon has started to shed its visible form. This energy is great for shedding rituals, banishing, and shadow work. Magic to do with shrinking, getting rid of, eliminating, deepening your work, retreating, looking within, and removing obstacles is best worked during this phase.

- *Half moon (first or third quarter):* when the moon is at full balance. The first and third quarters are both great for balancing rituals and magic, energy balancing, and anything else concerned with balance.

- *Waxing moon (getting larger):* when the moon is starting to grow larger. This energy is great for anything that requires manifestation on a larger scale—luck, love, and all the things you want to manifest. Use this time to "gain" energy, power, prosperity, luck, victory, etc.

- *New Moon (Dark Moon):* when the moon is completely hidden from our view. This energy is fantastic for planting seeds (physical and metaphorical),

final clearing, banishing, and endings that are followed by new beginnings. You can use the energy
right before the Dark Moon as "death energy" and
the energy right after it as "birth energy."

Exercise: Moon Gazing

Starting with the Full Moon, begin to watch the cycle
and phases of the moon. Each night, spend at least five to
ten minutes moon gazing. How does the Full Moon make
you feel? How does the Dark Moon feel? What types
of magic do you usually work during these phases? For
women, what is your own monthly cycle? Does it correspond with the moon's? If yes, how so? It is important
to note that, in the past, women's cycles often matched
those of the moon. In the modern world we live in, however, this is not the case, because ambient light and other
factors interfere. So do not feel as if you are lacking in
any way if your own cycle does not match the moon's.
Instead, try to journal your body's rhythm in compar-
ison to the moon's phases. What is your own personal
rhythm? Consider working a spell on the Full Moon of
each month (thirteen in all) or on the Dark Moon.

OCEAN TIDES

Tides are the rise and fall of the ocean caused by the gravitational pull of the moon. Ocean tide cycles occur every
12.5 hours, but every 6.5 hours there is a tidal change,

resulting in many different types of tides that are created by this gravitational pull. The moon's own cycles, as well as things like eclipses, have an effect on the ocean's tides.

Tides are also not exclusive to the ocean. Larger bodies of water and even lakes can show the effects of gravity's pull. In sea magic and witchcraft, witches learn the tides of their own bodies and of water so they can work with the intricate energies associated with the moon's pull. Where you are in the world will affect what time the tides around you rise and ebb. Once you have familiarized yourself with these tidal patterns, you can begin to work consciously with their energies. This work may include anything from doing spell work at a particular tide, to sending out offerings, aligning with astrological anomolies, calling on moon energy, and performing rituals at a certain time.

Below is a list of tides and how you can work with them magically (see figure 2 on page 164). It is important to consult your local tide table, however, as the tides are slightly different from one location to another.

- *Ebb tide:* the period between high and low tide when the water flows out. This tide is great for banishing work, getting rid of obstacles, sending things and people away, and movement. In Norfolk and Suffolk, it was believed that those born at ebb tide would face many challenges in life.

- *Flow or flood tide:* when the tide is coming in. This is a great time to work magic pertaining to creativity, creation, growth, expansion, and quickening. In Norfolk and Suffolk, it was believed that there were more children born when the tide was coming in.

- *High tide:* when the tide is at its greatest height. This occurs every 12.5 hours, and is a great time for prosperity magic and all types of magic pertaining to abundance.

- *Low tide:* when the tide is at its lowest. It is a great time to scavenge, and to "send out" any magic associated with banishing, shadow work, getting rid of unwanted things, cutting cords, and breaking habits.

- *Leeward tide:* when the tide and the wind flow in the same direction, in harmony.

- *Neap tide:* characerized by lower than normal water levels. These are the lower levels of high tide and can be used like a mild high tide. They occur when the moon is in the first and third quarters.

- *Spring tide:* not derived from the season, but from the verb "to spring," thus to jump up. These tides ebb and flow most powerfuly at the New and Full Moons and are characterized by higher than normal water levels. This tide can be used for any type of growth and expansion.

- *Windward tide:* when the wind and the tide flow and blow in opposition.

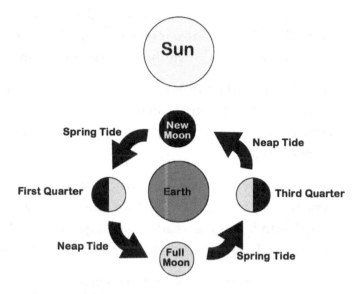

Figure 2: Tide cycles in relation to the sun and moon.

SHELLS

Working with seashells is probably one of my favorite forms of sea magic. I personally believe that we have a child-like connection to these amazing artifacts. Their diverse shapes and colors, and the creatures that live in them, lend themselves to an almost unlimited variety of magical workings. Seashells are actually the exo-skeletons of invertebrates. They consist primarily of calcium carbonate and about 2 percent protein. They are similar to bone, but, instead of creating an internal support structure, they create a bone-like shield. Thus any strong shell can be used for protection and shielding.

When selecting shells for use in your magic, it is important to note a few things. First, it is not legal or safe to collect shells at all beaches. Some beaches have strict rules about taking shells, sand, or water. Others are open for anyone to take what they please. When you collect shells on these beaches, however, check to make sure there are no living creatures inside them. Never take a live creature home—unless, of course, you are clamming for a delicious soup or fishing for dinner! This goes for other creatures like octopus, sand dollars, and starfish as well. If you find one washed up on the shore, it may not necessarily be dead and may just need to be taken back into the ocean. With our precious waters always under attack from harvesting and pollution, wise witches will value life and only take home that which the ocean has already given. Never take the life of an endangered creature.

Some argue that there are specific rites in which a live specimen can be used. That may well be, but that is a decision each witch must make. It is always wise not to offend the spirits of the water, for it can lead to catastrophic results. Always put the good of the water first and it will bless you abundantly in return. In chapter 7, you'll find ideas for appropriate offerings.

Shells have been used in every culture, and have specific meanings depending on the culture and use. The

Celts used mollusks as food, and the Scots incorporated periwinkle as part of their food supply. Later, during WWII, a luck charm using periwinkle is recorded. Cowrie shells were found in a seventh-century Anglo-Saxon burial chamber. There are reports of temples, graves, and other important ancient places being decorated with shells, and there are many burial pits and ceremonial places where shells have been found in abundance. In the 19th century, "conchylomania" ran rampant across the aristocratic societies of Europe. Many sea captains brought home boxes and trunks full of shells from their adventures around the world, trading them, selling them, or hoarding them as treasures. In one case, a shell was sold for $20,000!

Before that, a deep reverence and love for shells was found in most cultures. The black-lipped oyster was often used in carved jewelry, and for other, often magical, purposes as well. One report tells of a shell that was used as a magical thimble. Other shells were collected as charms and painted or carved with protection sigils, crosses, and other sacred symbols. These types of traditional charms were very individualized and unique to each practitioner. If you choose to use one, you should create it in accordance with your own practice. Oyster shells are often used in love spells, because they are thought to have aphrodisiac properties—especially if you are lucky enough to find a heart-shaped oyster. They can also be used for protection. One such charm found in the Boscastle Museum in Cornwall was used to protect against fire. The shell was painted with protection charms and laid in a black box.

Below is a list of magical, folkloric, and cultural uses of shells. These correspondences come from my own work—which is often, but not exclusively, based on European folklore—but their traditional sources and uses have been noted. Shells are diverse and vastly different, and, like stones and crystals, they can have multiple uses and meanings. By no means does this list represent the only way to work with shells. If you find a shell and it speaks to you with a specific meaning, listen to the spirit of the water rather than to correspondences found in any book—including this one. My goal is to help you build a practice of shell magic based on your own experience—with perhaps a little help from this book.

- *Cat's eye (turban shells)*: snail shells with a brown or white spiral on one side and muted colors on the other. Used in charms against the evil eye and for protection; sometimes called the eye of Saint Lucia and used in charms associated with luck.

- *Clam*: used for beauty, protection, money, abundance, love, purification, vitality, stability, and balance (or unbalance, if you have only one half).

- *Cockle*: used for love, purification, to banish negativity, centering, meditation, and new beginnings. In Skye, a cockleshell was floated in a pool of water surrounded by black stones when a witch intended to sink a ship.

- *Conch:* used for spirit communication, necromancy, and as a container for water or vase; also called the oracle shell.

- *Cowry:* used for burial rites, afterlife rites, offerings, goddess and fertility rites, prosperity and money charms, and workings related to eyes, seeing, the third eye, and the voice and eyes of the gods; also used to invoke good luck, protection from the evil eye, knowledge, song, wisdom, abundance, and growth.

- *Devil's toenails:* an extinct species of oyster that resembles a nautilus or snail shell. Carried as an amulet, it helped ease joint pain; powdered, it was used to ease back pain in horses. It can also be used as a stroking stone, but has its own correspondences and should not be used in substitution for a nautilus, snail, or ammonite shell, as they have their own specific uses.

- *Green ormer abalone:* used for stress relief, spiritual development, anxiety relief, luck, beauty, good fortune, ceremony, and cleansing. Abalone shells were not used by Europeans for smudging; however they make beautiful offering bowls. Closing the holes with beeswax turns this beautiful shell into a wonderful bowl to scoop charm water during cleansing rites or to hold water for saining with fresh bundled herbs.

- *Limpet:* used to increase power, invoke a cone of power, protection, empowerment, courage, and wisdom. They also make nice holders for stick incense.

- *Moon shell:* used for protection from the evil eye, moon cycles, and tides. It brings you closer to the sea and cleanses negative energies; it can be used for Mother Goddess and Full Moon rites.

- *Mussel:* used for rites involving stability, the moon, community, pearls, and food sources.

- *Oyster:* used for creation, binding, connecting to the moon, good fortune, beauty, and protection.

- *Periwinkle:* used for prosperity, health issues, friendship, integrity, and luck.

- *Scallop:* used for fertility, loyalty, love, and protection.

- *Slipper:* used for protection, dream promotion, relaxation, mysteries, hidden messages, communication, and nonconformity. This is an invasive species, so they are used well in spells that are about invading, spreading, taking over, fertility, and expansion.

- *Snail:* used for luck and longevity, protection from the evil eye, good luck, healing, and fertility. The Romany believed that these shells were very lucky, and any shell with a word naturally written on it was highly prized. They were sometimes strung and hung in the home for protection.

- *Wentletrap:* used for prosperity, purity, protection, meditation, peace, and moving forward.

- *Whelk:* used for taking control of a situation, decrees, and emotional stress. Much suspicion surrounded the whelk and it was believed unlucky to leave an empty whelk in the home overnight. They were also associated with the time from Christmas through Bride's Day (February 1st) and were cooked and eaten in soup.

- *Worm shell:* used to confuse and entangle enemies, to obtain knowledge and guidance, and to obtain a job. Groupings of them can be used to bring companions together; breaking them can be used to break free.

OTHER TREASURES OF THE SEA

The shore is a liminal place, and many gifts are deposited there by winds and tides. In addition, treasures are often found at the base of shoreline cliffs or tucked away in dunes. Fossils dot the cliffs of Lyme Regis, while giant megalodon teeth are found at the bottom of the Atlantic Ocean. Shells are found all over the world and sea beans travel the waves from shore to shore.

The ocean is mysterious and liminal—a portal to and part of the Otherworld. It also connects us to other cultures and places by bringing rare objects from far away to our local shores. Many of these items have a history of being used in magic, witchcraft, or folk charms. Below are some of the things that you can find and collect along the shore. If you find something not on this list, grab it anyway! You can always work with the object and find its meaning through meditation.

- *Amber:* a precious gift from the sea that can be strung on red thread for protection. The Scots used this as a protection charm.

- *Ambergris:* a wax-like substance that comes from the bowels of whales and is used for perfume and as an aphrodisiac. Once considered more valuable than gold, it can be used in love spells, sexual spells, and money-gaining spells.

- *Ammonite:* contains the primordial energy of the sea, ancestors, and cycles, similar to the nautilus. It can be used as a stroking stone, to remove cramps, for protection and fertility, to help reverse infertility, and for working with serpent or dragon energy. It can also be used in transference and healing.

- *Belemnite fossils:* fossils of ancient squid, an extinct order of cephalopods often thought to be associated with the Norse god Thor and thunderbolts. They are useful as blasting stones and, if hung around the neck, for protection. They were once called thunderbolts, and were believed to help protect against lightning strikes. Like ammonite, they were often mistakenly associated with serpents, being thought to be the tongues of ancient serpents. They can help protect from elfshot, a medical condition similar to arthritis believed to be caused by invisible elves shooting their victims with invisible arrows. (The term was also sometimes used to indicate a mysterious illness or condition.) These fossils can be used in general protection spells or as amulets to blast corporations that are destroying our waterways. They were used specifically to direct aggressive energy much as a blackthorn wand might do, and to ward or protect. They were also used more specifically in magic that harmed another, whether for a good reason or not.

- *Coral:* comes in many different forms and can be used for a variety of purposes, most commonly in magic and witchcraft for protection. It helps to protect and to ward off the evil eye. It can be used in sea necromancy, to alleviate madness and nightmares, and to protect against drowning. The Greeks believed black coral had medicinal qualities.

- *Crab shells and claws:* used for protection, withdrawal, and retreat.

- *Crinoid fossils:* also called sea lilies, sea stars, and victory stones. These are fossils of ancient sea creatures that are related to the starfish and sea urchin that were believed to bring victory to those who carried them. They are often found with belemnites, which fed on them. They sometimes occur naturally with holes in the center, making them very powerful hagstones as well. They may have been used as rosary beads as far back as the mid-13th century.

- *Driftwood:* can be used in wands and staffs, as talismans, and in charms. It is associated with transformation and endurance.

- *Fisher floats (witch balls):* used for protection and to trap energy. Coins were placed in cork floats as payment to the sea gods in exchange for a good catch.

- *Fishing nets:* can be used for catching or entangling an enemy, for binding, and for prosperity.

- *Hagstones:* used for a wide variety of purposes, including protection, for magic, to bring psychic visions, or as a window into the Otherworld. They are most often used for protection hung on a red cord or string.

- *Heart-shaped stones or shells:* considered auspicious in the realms of love, romance, and relationships, but also for protection. They can be used in sympathetic magic to heal the heart or blood diseases.

- *Mary's bean (Airene Mhoire):* used as a charm in childbirth to ease pain. It was also given to teething babies in Ireland, and can be used as a protective amulet when worn around the neck.

- *Mother of pearl:* can be used in healing spells and charms. It is often associated with mermaids, dreamtime, and relaxation.

- *Orthoceras:* another fossil that can be used in magic. Today, many use it in healing rites. Modern witches use it as a protective talisman, but it can be used successfully in ways similar to belemnite. It also has an interesting connection to the sympathetic healing of the spine.

- *Pearls:* formed from a tiny imperfection inside a mollusk while it tries to repair itself. Thus pearls are the direct result of healing energy and can be used as such. They are associated with June and moon children and are intimately connected to the moon in magical practices, as they resemble it in shape, luster, and color. Pearls can be used to make beauty and healing essences and can be given as offerings to spirits, goddesses, and the sea. They can be used in wisdom magic, and in any magic associated with the astrological sign of Cancer, the moon, or crabs. They are also used in transformation magic through sympathetic association as a prized gem created from a tiny flaw. They are great in spells involving transformation, beauty, the Goddess, Venus, empowerment, and rejuvenation, and are used in spells related to drought, health, sexual potency, and healing.

- *Pebbles and stones:* white for healing; black for protection and transference.

- *Sand:* gray and black sand for protection, banishing, and nocturnal magic; white or lighter-colored sand for healing spells; wet brown sand to connect with sea energies, grounding, and prosperity. You can also use the time of day, tide, and weather to influence the sand. Sun-drenched sand collected on the equinox is different from sand taken from a beach during a storm at high tide. Label your sand with the date, the moon cycle, and the energy surrounding it before you bottle it up.

- *Sand dollar:* associated with the pentagram, money, divine inspiration, wholeness, and prosperity.

- *Sea coal:* coal that has been in the ocean and, like sea glass or pebbles, worn down by the sea and deposited on the shore. These pieces have been used in charms to protect from evil spirits, to protect a boat from dangers at sea, and for good fortune.

- *Sea glass:* can be used in spells involving transformation, the death/rebirth cycle, and in color magic.

- *"Fossilized" saw-fish snout:* used in divination to carve out lines in the sand upon which shells and other items are cast; also called mermaids' combs.

- *Sea beans:* used for rites involving new life, childbirth, seeds of wisdom, and travel. They are described in Iceland as being sacred to Freyja, and have been carried and worn for prosperity. They are also called sea nuts, strand nuts, and faery eggs, and were thought to cure sick cattle and protect from the evil eye.

- *Seahorse:* used for protection, to avert the evil eye, and for luck. It is best to find these on the beach naturally, or to purchase one from a beach comber if you are sure it was found washed up with the tide. Be careful, because many places farm them for decorations. It is much better to accept a real one that has been washed up as a gift from the sea. If you want to work with a seahorse and you don't have a real one, you can use a charm, image, or piece of ceramic that is shaped like one.

- *Sea urchin:* when fossilized, this is called a faery loaf. It is used in prosperity, money, and protection charms.

- *Seaweed:* used for fertility, prosperity, mermaid magic, binding, healing, and nourishment.

- *Shark and marine teeth:* used for protection, aggressive magic, and animal associations. They were thought to provide good protection against poison when worn as an amulet.

- *Sailor's purse:* also called sea purse, mermaid's purse, or maid's purse. These are egg pouches from a shark, skate, or a sting ray that was birthed at sea. These are also called devil's purses, which hints at their powerful nature in spell work. You can find them on the shore of almost any beach, usually mixed in among washed-up seaweed. They make perfect vessels for magic that involves growth, prosperity, fertility, birth, and renewal. They can also be used for protection, especially by a mother who is casting to protect her child.

- *Starfish:* used for weather magic, pentagram, opportunity, and regeneration.

SEAWEED

Seaweed is a delicious snack and has been used across the world in culinary dishes. Most ocean seaweed is edible; however some conditions may change that and some types may be more suited for eating than others. Algae from ponds and lakes, on the other hand, is usually not safe to ingest. In Ireland, seaweed is traditionally cooked into soup. At one point, it was collected and highly prized as a source of iodine.

Seaweed is quite useful in sea magic as well. It can be used for protection from evil spirits, according to a highland belief that evil spirits can't go below the tide line. Bladderwrack is used in both ancient and modern sea spells, and it can be useful in working with mermaids, attracting money, and for protection if carried as a protective talisman while traveling over the sea or ocean. It is also often used to summon sea spirits. A type called dead man's fingers can be used in necromancy, binding, and ancestral spirit work. Dulse is useful in magical cooking, and in longevity and prosperity rituals. Irish Moss (*Chondrus crispus*) is useful for grounding, and is used in raw culinary dishes and skin products. It can be used magically in the same way. Sea tangle (*Laminaria digiata*) is useful in binding or trapping. Kelp is great for travel, protection, and money spells, and can also be used in binding. A black seaweed is described in folklore as something that entangled witches, or something mermaids used to drown sailors and strangle men.

Sea grass (not to be confused with seaweed) can be used as you would regular grass in fiber magic and in cord or knot magic, and provides a home and breeding area for seahorses. Meillich (milearch, or sea-matweed) was associated with faery cows and believed by some to be where they lived. In the western islands of the UK, a practice was used to call wrack to shore when there was little seaweed coming in. A large bowl of porridge made with hearty ingredients and butter was poured out on each headland. The next day, the harbors were full. The idea was that the porridge would send bounty from the land into the sea; in return, the bounty or fruit of the sea came to land.

TRADITIONAL OCEAN CHARMS

There are many types of charms that are related to the sea, and an almost unlimited number if you think of all the uses that can be made of the gifts from the sea. Here, we'll focus on a few that are traditional to the Celts and Britons, and to their descendants.

Fish are useful for many things. Certain bones were used in charms, as we have already seen, but live fish can be used in transference as well. As with stones, a fish can be rubbed on the body of someone who is sick, then thrown back into the ocean, taking the transferred disease with it. To uncross a vessel that was cursed and unable to catch fish, fishermen pierced a mackerel with pins or nails and placed it in the stern.

Coral is used largely for protection and luck, while amber washed ashore and strung on red silk was worn by upper-class women as an amulet. Crab and lobster claws were used in protection charms and to bring in a good catch of fish. One such working found in the collection of the Museum of Witchcraft and Magic in Boscastle, Cornwall, includes a charm written on paper and then tucked inside the claw, which was then carefully sealed and either worn or hung in a boat. Crab shells were used in charms to take revenge on an unfaithful lover. The shells were broken and ground into a powder, then mixed into the target's next meal to ensure that the marriage would remain happy and the unfaithful partner would return. Cat's eye, or turban shells, were used in charms against the evil eye, and were useful for protection as well.

Those that were born in a caul were said to have the ability to tell fortunes and be immune from drowning. Cauls were often dried and sold to sailors and those traveling overseas as a magical charm to protect the wearer from drowning. Numerous charms of saints have been used to protect sailors as well, and graveyard dirt from particular saints' graves was considered to protect them from harm. In a ritual from the Shetlands, aspiring witches went down to the seashore at night. Lying down under the tide line with their left hand under their feet and their right hand on their heads, they said an enchantment similar to this three times: "The muckel master devil will take what is between these two hands."

Shells—usually cowrie and snail shells—were used to protect from the evil eye, especially in children. Wood, cork, and glass fisher floats were used as well, and glass fisher floats (or witch balls) were often hung in a witch's window to catch baneful energy and evil spirits. These needed to be watched closely when used in this manner, however, because if they became dull or tarnished, it foretold ill fortune or sickness. Silver coins were placed in cork floats and offered as payment to the sea gods. If the coin disappeared, the payment had been accepted; if not, the gods were apparently not in need of the payment or offering.

The charms associated with sea magic varied widely and touched on all phases of life on both land and sea. An Orcadian witch charm states that three handfuls of sea water placed in a pail and added to a butter churn will bring prosperity and a good production. The pelt and right front paw of an otter were considered protective and were used as talismans by sailors. A Mary bean or Malaga nut from Brazil, as well as white hagstones, were considered auspicious and thought to bring good favor to seamen. Sailors from the Isle of Man kept wren feathers in their pockets or purses to keep the mer and fair folk away. In Clonmany, the villagers drove their cattle into the sea near where a sacred spring flowed into it. In Scotland, the same was done with horses on Lammas tide, possibly as a purification or cleansing rite. Red thread was used in Scotland to hang hagstones that could ward off the evil eye; in Wales, amber was used in a similar manner. Red coral and rowan berries strung on red thread were worn in Scotland as a protective amulet.

In Britain, horseshoes were said to enchant boats and ships in several ways. A horseshoe nailed to the mast of a boat with the ends pointed up was believed to bring luck and good fortune. If the ends pointed down, it was believed to protect from evil spirits. A horsehoe nailed to the mast of a ship was used to protect it from witches' enchantments and to bring luck. They were used to protect both house boats and sea-going vessels, and were also placed at the end of boat ramps to keep evil spirits off the boats moored there. Today, we can use them to protect our cars—our land vessels. Hagstones can be used in a similar way, often tied with red thread.

Scottish witches used wooden bowls and seashells to work weather magic. They set the shells afloat on the water in the bowl, then stirred the water to produce gale conditions. In some areas, black cats were associated with storms as well and were feared for their ability to bring dangerous weather. On the other hand, in Scarborough, the wives of fishermen and sailors kept a black cat to ensure that their mates would be safe at sea. It was believed that witches traveled on the sea in eggshells, so eggshells were considered lucky for sailors and believed to protect them from enchantments and drowning if carried in their pockets. In Wales, hanging a bundle of seaweed by the back door warded off evil; in Cornwall, bunches of seaweed hung in the chimney protected the home from fire. Fishermen carried salt to deter witches, while oyster shells were believed to have miraculous attributes and were worn around the neck as a cure for croup in children.

Sea urchins—also called faery loafs, shepherd's crown, or thunder stones—sport a pentagram-like motif on the top, and were used in magical work in Suffolk by placing them on the mantel to ensure there would always be bread in the home. Sometimes they were placed in a bakery to produce a good supply of bread. They were also used to protect against lightning, to keep milk from souring, and poisons. The Romans wore them as amulets, and they have been found in graves and burial chambers. They have also been used to ward off evil spirits, protect against witchcraft, and as a charm against drowning. In East Anglia, they were used to protect from evil enchantments, poverty, and storms. You were considered very lucky if you found one.

SEA SPELLS AND CHARMS

Spells and charms that work with the powers of ocean waters have played a part in many cultures and folk traditions around the world. These often call upon the properties of sea creatures; conversely, these spells are often used to protect those same creatures and the seas they swim in. A good example of this is the spell used to protect dolphins given at the end of this chapter.

Dolphins are an incredibly intelligent species that is honored in many traditions. In fact, in India, dolphins were recently given status as non-person humans to protect them from being captured and slaughtered. Unfortunately, in other parts of the world, dolphins are still hunted for sport. Dolphins have been known to rescue sailors who are lost at sea or from a shipwreck. One story tells of a sailor who speared a dolphin and suddenly encountered a wild water man who took him to another land. There, he found his victim, now a knight, with the sailor's spear still stuck in him. The dolphin forgave the sailor and, from that day on, dolphins were honored on the sea. It is still believed to be very unlucky to kill one. In magic, dolphins are associated with communication, echo location, sound, breath, creation, passion, sexuality, healing, and manifestation.

Below is just a sampling of some of the rites and charms performed by sea witches to honor and protect the sea, and to call upon its power in their magic.

- *Charm to capture and release the wind:* This old charm describes sailors purchasing knots from witches who had captured the wind so they could use them while at sea. It involves dipping a rope that has been used out at sea into water from the ocean nine times, then tying three knots in it during a wind storm or on a gusty day. The first knot was enchanted to produce a light breeze, the second to produce a moderate wind, and the third to call up a strong gale. In Scotland, sailors sometimes purchased a handkerchief that was prepared in the same way from witches that specialized in air or wind magic. The power of the charm relies on capturing the wind in the knotted rope or fabric and storing it for later use. As each knot was undone, it released its power, but could not be used again. So sailors had to purchase a new rope or handkerchief for subsequent voyages—good employment security for witches specializing in wind magic.

- *Spell to banish:* Village folk use this incantation to rid themselves of harmful or troublesome influences and send them out to sea. They repeated the words "Out and away" three times, followed by the words " To the sea," spoken three times.

- *A modern spell to bind companies that harm the water:* To bind companies that harm our oceans, place their logo inside a clam or oyster shell. Wrap the shell with bindweed, tangled seaweed, or a fisherman's net. On the waning moon, take it to a place where three rivers meet and bury it near where they intersect, calling upon the local spirits to aid you. You can also take the shell to a crossroads, preferably by a graveyard, and leave it in the center. In either case, walk away and don't look back.

- *Protection charm for traveling over water:* Find an oyster shell or scallop that has both sides intact. Inside it, place a bit of your hair, a garnet, and a small piece of amber; then bind it all together with red thread. Sprinkle the shell with holy water of your choice and tuck it into your suitcase, pocket, or purse.

- *Sand spell for protection:* Sand spells are easy and fun to use. This spell uses either darker or gray/black sand for protection. On the day after the Dark Moon (the New Moon), gather your dark sand and pour it into a jar, filling it one quarter to half-way full. Place a taglock or image of what you want to protect in the jar; for added protection, try adding some black stones, or black tourmaline. Fill the jar to the top with sand and seal it with black wax or a black cloth. Charge it under the energy of the New Moon for seven days. When the jar is fully charged, speak your intent over a bowl of sea water while dipping the sealed jar into the water seven times.

- *Healing spell for the water:* So much of our water today is being polluted and the creatures that live within it are constantly in danger. This powerful spell can be used anywhere to protect and tend waters that need protection. Select a tumbled quartz crystal and

charge it every day under a New Moon as it grows
to full. You can also whisper incantations of healing
over the stone and charge it with healing energy.
On the Full Moon, take the stone to the ocean and
wade out far enough so that nine waves can flow
past you. Cast the stone into the water, reciting this
incantation:

Spirits of the Sea
I am here to heal thee;
With my power
And my will,
 I calm these waters
And make them still.
Still to heal and to calm,
Heal to clean, clean to heal.
These waters are sacred, blessed,
And flow clean at will.

- *Sand spell for healing:* On the Full Moon, gather white
  sand and fill a jar one quarter to half-way full. Place
  your taglock in the jar and add some blue or white
  stones for healing—aquamarine, blue-lace agate,
  blue calcite, selenite, rainbow moonstone, or quartz.
  Fill up the jar with sand and seal it with blue wax or
  a blue cloth. Charge it under the energy of the Full
  Moon for three days—the entire Full Moon period.
  Then, speaking your intent, dip the sealed jar into a
  bowl of sea water nine times.

- *Sea spell for prosperity:* For this rite, you will need a mermaid's purse (see above). Write your intent on paper, being specific about the type of prosperity you want and how you want to achieve it. Roll the paper up and tuck it gently inside the egg case. Paint or draw a symbol on top that represents prosperity—for instance, the Norse rune *Fehu.* You can speak incantations as you do this, then seal the pouch with wax and consecrate it with sea water. Set the charm on your altar or shrine space and recharge it every few moon cycles. The energies of the mermaid's purse will combine with the fierceness of the animal, the power of the sigil, the symbolism of the egg pouch, and the power of your spoken words to create a power-packed charm.

- *Ninth-wave spell for healing:* This is a quick and effective spell for light healing work—one I often use to "reset" when I'm not feeling like myself. Just go to the beach and wade into the water deep enough so that nine consecutive waves can wash over most of your body. Count the waves as you sense their cleansing power. At the ninth wave, state your intent and ask to be healed.

Exercise: Protect the Dolphins

To complete this rite, you will need:

- 1 black candle (Try to use soy or beeswax and stay away from paraffin, as it is harmful to the environment.)

- Pointy and sharp shell shard(s)

- A black cloth bag

- A charm, photo, ornament, or statue of a dolphin, or some other icon that denotes a dolphin

Carve the word "dolphin" into the wax of your candle with the shell shard. If you want to protect whales, write that, or the name of any other creature instead. When you are ready to cast the spell, take the candle to the ocean and, keeping the wick dry, dip it into the water three times. Dig a little hole in the dry sand deep enough to protect the candle's flame from any sea breezes and place the candle in it. Light the candle and let it burn down until it is just a little puddle of wax in the hole. While it burns, focus your intent on the ocean and on the dolphins living there. When the candle is completely burned down, take the melted wax, the sand that surrounds it, and any other sharp shells you find and tuck them into the bag with the icon of the dolphin. Wade back into the water and, with your dominant hand, sprinkle the bag with ocean water from the third wave that washes over you; then send out your final intent. Take the protection charm back to your home and place it on your workspace. Be sure to charge it and feed its energy regularly.

Chapter 7

Local Water Spirits

The spirits that inhabit natural places are referred to as *genius loci*, which is Latin for "spirit of place" or "guardian of place." The term is frequently used to describe local flora and fauna and the spirits that reside on or in the water, reflecting an animistic view that everything possesses a soul. We know that nature has many mysteries still waiting to be discovered and that trees communicate through local fungi networks. These plants and many others have always been sacred to and played a large part in the natural witch's path. But while plants hold the energy of the earth, the earth holds the water. And without water, there would be no life. The elements of water and earth are thus intimately connected and rely on each other to support all life forms. And because there are many plants that grow in soil in or around water sources, there are many stories about water spirits who dwell within the trees along sacred shores and springs.

I used to get very caught up in having the right formula for a spell, or crafting with the correct natural correspondences or tools. But when I started to explore my path in depth and became more confident in it, I found that these were only references and context, and not the work itself. The most important thing that we can learn from nature is not lists of associations or correspondences given to us by others; the most important thing we can learn is to listen to the genius loci—to the spirits, plants, and creatures that dwell there. Books are very helpful and can be a great place to start. But witches have to get their hands dirty and learn from their own experiences.

When working in your local enviornment, make sure that it is safe and legal to harvest the plants, stones, sand, and shells you may need for your craft. Some places have strict rules or restrictions on harvesting plants, shells, and sand from the shores, while others may have none. It is always important to comply with the local laws, which, after all, were put in place to protect the local environment and preserve our beautiful beaches, lakes, and rivers, not to infringe on our magical freedoms. Beach dunes, for instance, may be closed to protect turtles that breed there, or to preserve plants that are necessary to keep them from eroding.

There will almost certainly be lots of wonderful local growth around your water source, and it is important to "know" your plants. Take a camera with you when you explore your local waters; take photographs and sketch the stem structure, leaves, and flowers of the plants you find. This will help you avoid mixing up plants, which can be dangerous. For example, Queen Anne's lace, which grows well in marshland, looks quite similar to water hemlock, which is a deadly poison. Water hemlock also grows well along the ocean shores and in wetlands. Take a reliable field guide with you as you learn to work with plants, and plan on making several exploratory trips before you begin your workings—one to observe, photograph, and sketch; one to harvest sample plants and take them home to identify them; and one to gather the plants you have researched that you will need for your magic.

If you find an area that is safe to harvest, it is a good rule to take only a quarter of any plant and never take the last one. If you are unable to identify a specific plant, it is better to leave it where it is. Chances are it is not the right magical tool, spirit, or medicine for you at that time. When a plant spirit wants to work with you, it will make itself known to you in strange and mysterious ways! Make sure to bring an offering with you—perhaps natural ethical food for the local animals, if that is allowed—along with charged pebbles, any blessed water you have been working with, and a bag to clean up trash.

VISITING WATER

Practitioners of water magic must develop a personal relationship with water. As a watery person, you will most likely want to visit the water sources around you, if you haven't already done so. There are natural wonders around us everywhere, and many unique water sources. Even in the hottest deserts, there are hot springs, waterfalls, and rivers. Research the types of water sources in and around your location. Look at beaches, sacred wells, rivers, lakes, springs, ponds, and pools; then find out which ones allow visitors and when you can visit. Examine their rules and regulations. Then plan a trip to one, or to as many as you like. Use the exercise below to begin to connect with the local water spirits. Try visiting on both the Full and New Moons, and plan on doing a meditation each time you are there. Bring an offering of some sort, using the list of proper and ethical offerings below to determine what is best—food for the birds, flowers for the waters, or other organic offerings for the wildlife that inhabits the place. In chapter 9, you will learn how to make elixirs, flower waters, teas, and hydrosols, some of which make good offerings.

Even if you bring the proper offerings, however, you still need to take precautions. You will be trying to establish a working relationship with a body of water and will want to take water from it in the future, so you must show the waters that you are not just taking from them, but that you are bringing something to the relationship as well. Spend time cleaning the area and caring for the water to show that you are not just there for your own selfish reasons and that you deeply care about the local spirits and life that dwell there. You are most likely dealing with a sacred source of water with a long history and great power. Do not try to dominate it. Rather, set out to establish a symbiotic relationship with it.

Bring a blanket or something to help you become comfortable in the place. I bring a basket that has smaller baskets inside it in which I can carry my offerings to the water. If the waters are willing and allow me to take things in return, I carry them home in this same basket. It is important to consider the word "sacrifice" here. When you take things from the water, the water is giving of itself to you. In return, you must give back a piece of yourself or some other sacrifice. Hair is a good offering, as birds use it to build their nests. I once offered some hair to a hummingbird and she used it to repair her nest. It was amazing to watch her weave the thin strands to pull her nest back together and secure it delicately to the branch. Sacrifice is a difficult concept, but it has some very important lessons to teach us. Always remember to give before you take; and never take without permission.

COLLECTING WATER

Water can be collected anywhere. Even in the driest environments, you can find sacred springs and pools. Or perhaps you will collect your water from a manmade fountain in your favorite city, or from a well on a sacred pilgrimage. I have a small vial of water that I collected from a fount in Salem that is among my favorite tools. Or you may collect water from your neighborhood pond or creek. Just be careful about the water you collect and put your health first. If you don't already have a stash of jars and bottles, now is a good time to gather some, as you will need to start bottling up different types of water, potions, and elixirs.

Before you begin to collect water, there are a few things to keep in mind and a few things to beware. Remember, there is no one proper way to collect water from different locations. Start with a good labeling system. Everyone may have a different method, but everyone needs to know what is in their bottles. Some like to write directly on their containers, others use stickers, and some simply use tape and a marker. I use beautiful labels that I created myself. These are blank, so that I can quickly grab one and label a container whenever I need to. There is nothing worse than collecting water, failing to label it, and then staring at the jars for hours trying to remember which one is which!

Water witches tend to collect many different types of water from many different sources. After a while, you may find that you need a special cabinet just to hold your different waters and elixirs. In the end, all these bottles will look alike, so when you collect water, be sure to bring your labels and pen with you! It is also helpful to record the location from which the water is taken, the water type, the day and time you collected it, the moon cycle, the planetary hour, and any auspicious astrological correspondences. Water collected from different locations at different times will have its own unique energy signature. Salt water is different from brackish water, which is different from frozen lake water, which is different still from water collected during a thunderstorm. Water from a city may be polluted, while water from a country sun shower may be a useful tool in healing magic. Spring water, on the other hand, can be bottled and used in rituals and baths, or even for drinking in some cases. Be sure to record any feelings, thoughts, or correspondences that you pick up as well.

The type of bottle or jar you select is also important. I highly recommend not storing your magical waters in plastic, as many bottles contain BPH, which is known to cause cancer. Your magic deserves a better container. Metal bottles or jars are a good choice, but they can rust. In my opinion, glass is probably the best type of bottle for storing your water, although I admit that, when transporting water over long distances in a suitcase or sending it by mail, it may be better to use plastic bottles temporarily, as they are lighter and less likely to break. Try to transfer the water into glass as soon as you can, however. Also note that, if you are using a mason jar with a metal lid, you may want to cover the lid with wax paper or not fill the jar to the top so the water doesn't touch the metal, as it may rust. Corked bottles are great for storing water, but they do not do well in transport. As I have found, they leak and you may lose your precious cargo.

You may also find that, after a while, certain types of water grow duckweed or other green aquatic matter. If this happens, don't worry—the water is not lost! You may not be able to drink it, but it is still useful in magic. I have a bottle of water—probably my most precious bottle—that is over five years old. I collected it from Llyn y Fan Fach when I was in Wales. I drove for three hours and then hiked for another three to get to it, and now I can't drink it. But I still use it to connect with the Gwragedd Annwn and the Lady of the Lake.

To collect water, first gather any votive offerings or ritual items you want to bring. Then venture out to your body of water. Find a nice spot to connect with the water and sit down by it. If it is a well, you may choose to sit near it. If it is the ocean, you may choose to sit on the beach. If you are at a lake, perhaps find a good place to sit that is quiet and away from activity. If the weather is warm, walk down to the shore and connect with the water. Observe all the creatures in and around the water and gaze at the surface. Is it calm or are there waves? What types of plants grow around it? What can it teach you?

After you have spent a considerable amount of time getting to know the water (and if it is safe and legal to do so), make your offering to the local spirits. It is important not to bring dyed or store-bought flowers full of chemicals to the water. These can harm the water and the spirits that live there. If you grow your own flowers or know of a place to get clean, natural, chemical-free blooms, by all means bring them to the water! Be mindful, however, that hundreds of flowers strewn upon the water can be messy. And remember that the offering must benefit the genius loci. If you can't find a suitable offering, try singing, chanting, drumming, reading a poem, or drawing sigils in the sand. Those that walk a shadow path may wish to offer bone, blood, or hair. Rather than putting these into the water as the ancient Celts did, perhaps bury them near the water, but far enough away to avoid contaminating it with bodily fluids.

Once you have connected with the water and given your votive offerings, make your way back to your quiet place, close your eyes, and enter into a light meditative state. Use all your senses to connect with the water—listen, breathe in the air, feel the air on your skin. Now bring your focus to your mind's eye and open your mind to the spirit of the water in front of you. Let your mind wander along the banks, across the surface, below the surface, and deep into the darkest places hidden within the depths of the water. Begin to speak with the water; tell the spirits there about yourself—who you are and what you intend. Ask if they would like to connect with you. Ask them to show you images or any messages they may want to share with you. Ask if they will begin to work with you, and if they will give you permission to take water or other natural objects found on the bank away with you.

If the answer is yes, come back to your body and into a present state. Walk along the banks and see if you find anything significant. If the answer was no, then you must establish more trust. Come back at a later date and try again, or perhaps rethink your offerings. Sometimes the spirits of a place just need time to get to know you and to learn to trust you, so have patience and know that they will eventually work with you. Once they see that you are willing to do the hard work and aren't like most humans who try to abuse, exploit, and pollute the environment, they will be willing to work with you.

OFFERINGS TO WATER

Almost all practices that surround magic and spirit work encourage or require a sacrifice or offering. Of course, the water has given us so much that it is only natural that we want to give back. Before giving, however, it is important for us as witches to dig deep down into our own personal wells of wisdom and examine our hearts. We must be sure that the offerings we are giving are truly votive offerings and beneficial to the environment.

The Celts and our ancestors often deposited large offerings into the water—swords, shields, even chariots. It would clearly be impractical to drive your car into the local lake as an offering to the water spirits, however.

So we must consider that not all modern equivalents of ancient votive offerings are appropriate in our day and age. Lead curse tablets like those found in Sulis Temple could be very harmful to local wildlife if deposited in a lake or small well. Consider instead using natural clay (not synthetic) tablets that can be buried, returning the earth back to the earth. Avoid introducing anything that is not natural into the waters around you.

I identify three different categories of votive offerings that I suggest you consider before making any offerings to the waters:

- *Positive-impact offerings:* This type of offering includes work that benefits the location and wildlife—items or actions that support ocean conservation, ocean animal advocacy, wildlife protection, and even binding corporations. It also includes actions like cleaning up beaches and rivers, rescuing stranded animals, and volunteering to help mitigate oil spills. You can even use energy healing on a regular basis to charge and heal the waters, or draw calming patterns in the sand, or arrange rocks in sacred patterns. Performing protection spells for the water and the creatures that live there, and creating healing potions for the ocean are meaningful offerings as well. You can even collect water and work with it for an entire moon cycle, then bring it back as a gift. This type of offering focuses on good works and deeds that specifically benefit the water. The key is to leave nothing behind and to leave the place better than you found it. These kinds of offerings can be given at any time.

- *No-impact offerings:* These focus on having a positive energetic, rather than a physical, impact. They leave no votive offerings or foreign objects behind, and use only the objects of nature. For example, you may collect driftwood, carve it with sacred symbols, charge it with magic, and then give it back to the shore. This introduces nothing harmful, but offers a small positive change to the local environment. You can also charge tumbled, undyed stones like agate, jasper, and quartz and leave them to help the energy of the place. Stones like these are found at many water sources, so it will not upset the natural balance of a place to mingle them with the stones naturally found there. Use wisdom and don't introduce stones that have been dyed, heat-treated, or unethically mined. Do not use paints, stains, or chemicals on any stone or driftwood. Ask yourself this simple question: Will this harm the animals, spirits, and plants that live here? If the answer is no, proceed; if the answer is yes, reconsider.

- *Low-impact offerings:* These are offerings that leave foreign objects as gifts to the spirits of a place. You must make sure, however, that these votive offerings do not in any way harm the water or the environment around it. This category includes things like clay effigies, flowers, and stones like aquamarine and amethyst that may not normally be found in an area. It also includes taglocks like hair, clooties, or unbleached paper that is 100 percent natural. Never choose items that contain dyes, pesticides, or chemicals, or that have been heat-treated. And never use plastic—*period*. It is better to bring a natural ethical offering than to bring a beautiful plastic object and suffer the wrath of the water spirits. Humans are so messy, disruptive, and disrespectful. If you want to be an ally to the genius loci, you must be wise and work for its good. It is your responsibility to know what you are adding to the water and the environment. Ignorance is no excuse! This type of offering should be reserved for special rites, spells, and auspicious days. If you are unsure, you can always ask the genius loci for advice.

Exercise: Choosing an Offering

Spend time in meditation. What types of positive- or no-impact offerings can you regularly give to the water? What do you have time to create? What brings you pleasure, but is also beneficial to the water? Make a list of offerings that fit into these categories. Then work with your local spirits to find out what they like and appreciate the most.

Exercise: Raising and Contacting Spirits

Raising and contacting water spirits is quite complicated. The first thing to keep in mind is that the work must be done in a cleansed, sacred, and protected space. Below you will find various cleansing and circle-casting techniques that can help you prepare these spaces.

You will also use the grounding technique given in chapter 2—both before and after you work any type of magic. In the case of spirit contact, casting a circle or laying a compass can both be used to create protective circles. As we have seen, water spirits, and spirits in general, may be either benevolent or malevolent, depending on the spirit and the day it is contacted. Even if you connect deeply with a spirit and have worked with it for some time, it is always important to protect yourself. And this goes for both the Judaic and Christian deities as well, who have a long history of violence.

To contact a water spirit, first prepare your ritual items and space, and your body. Be sure that your ritual space is clean and your ritual items set up, and that you have showered or taken a ritual bath. This applies if you are working in nature as well. Rather than dusting your ritual room and shrines, be sure to remove any trash and debris from your outdoor working space. Then spend some time grounding and shielding (see chapter 2). Pick your favorite method and use it.

Use your sacred water to cleanse the space—perhaps using a method found in this book—then cast a circle.

If you have a preferred method, use it; if not, use one of the suggestions below. Stand or sit within your cleansed sacred space, and begin to breathe in a rhythmic manner to bring yourself to a light trance state. This may take some practice or additional training. You may want to think about seeking out a local teacher at your local metaphysical shop.

When you feel as if you have altered your consciousness, bring your attention to your mind's eye. This is where you will first make contact with the spirit. Some more advanced practices call the spirit to the mundane realm, while others may have you cross a hedge or part a mist to make contact. In this exercise, you will meet the spirit in the in-between realm that can be viewed and interacted with in your mind. This can be a precursor to astral travel, so even if this practice seems simple, practicing it will increase your knowledge and help you to move naturally into other more advanced practices.

If you are by a lake, river, or ocean in your mind's eye, dive down and explore the underwater realms. Perhaps the spirit will meet you on the beach, or in your ritual room. Spend time learning about the spirit. What is its name? Is this its true name? Most often, these spirits will not give you their true names as that gives you power over them. Keep this in mind in the reverse as well! What does the spirit look like? Is it interested in you? What kinds of questions did you ask? Did the spirit ask you any?

If you can't travel to a physical body of water to perform this exercise, remember that water is everywhere—even in your own kitchen sink. You can hold a vial of water or a handful of sand from your favorite beach while sitting in your ritual or meditation space, and connect to the water spirits in that way. It may you take several tries, or you may have success right away. Try exploring different types of water, perhaps by having a friend send you water from another region or country, or from a beloved childhood beach. You can also use a shell to connect with water if you are land-locked.

Chapter 8

Mermaids and Finfolk

As we have seen from some of the folktales given in previous chapters, mermaids are beautiful—but they can be dangerous. They are often found lurking at the edge of the ocean, near a river, or in a quiet lake waiting to lure men to their deaths. They are not generally associated with fountains, although Melusine was an exception to this rule.

Mermaids are fascinating creatures that have generated a wide variety folklore in just about every culture around the world. They range from single-tailed merfolk to double-tailed sirens like Melusine—or even salmon-tailed spirits like Liban (see below). They have been depicted as both demons and saints. Many faery women and mermaids were, in fact, venerated as saints—for example, Saint Serena—and their sacred waters were often renamed after saints. Mermaids have been recorded since antiquity and many are considered to be either deities or demi-gods. They have been the subject of the visual arts, music, and poetry, and painters like

Waterhouse and other Pre-Raphaelites, as well as poets like Tennyson, have portrayed these beautiful water creatures in their artistic works.

It is my belief that the recent popularity of mermaids is rooted directly in our collective consciousness. We instinctively know mermaids exist, so we try to form a solid connection with them. There are too many sightings over great spans of time and across many cultures to ignore reports of mermaids or simply brush them off as folklore. The Celts, like the Greeks and Romans, had a deep belief in these beings, which were frequently recorded in folktales that were then passed from generation to generation, right up to our modern day.

Merfolk live in the darkest depths of the ocean, away from human influence. Like the faery folk, they have retreated beyond the veil, but are still able to pass between this world and the Otherworld, although that rarely happens today. These water spirits were so important to the Celts that both the Romans and the Christians could never completely erase them from the popular consciousness. So they simply tried to reframe the tales and make many of them part of the new cultures and religions they brought.

Some merfolk take on the classical look of a mermaid, while others may sport scaly bodies and green skin, or be translucent. Moroever, not all water spirits can be classified as merfolk. It is also important to note that many folktales describe these beings as malevolent, mischievous, or selfish—primarily those that fit the classic description of mermaids or lake faeries. Even the romantic Pre-Raphaelites portrayed their watery nature as both beautiful and deadly, as seen in *La Belle Dame sans Merci*.

It is true that some reports tell of captured merfolk who have granted wishes. But they also have a long history of sinking ships and taking men to their watery deaths. On the other hand, we have stories of benevolent Lake Ladies and merfolk like Melusine, who was very helpful to those she loved, as was the Lady of Llyn Y Fan Fach (see chapters 3 and 4). Likewise, the Gwragedd Annwn are interested in healing and helped feed villages with the milk of their faery cows. I personally think it is dangerous, however, to ignore folklore and historical references and make naïve and unguided attempts to interact with merfolk. One misstep, and they can create mischief and havoc.

Our obsession with merfolk continues today. Some purchase expensive tails to wear in the water, or adorn themselves with cutesy plastic flowers and rainbow-colored shell bras. While these may be amusing, however, they are not a way to transform yourself into a mermaid. Merfolk, Lake Ladies, and other finfolk belong to the spirit realm and often to the faery world, and no amount of wanting to be a mermaid will turn you into one. They are real and individual spirits that dwell in the realms of the Otherworld. They don't wear bathing suits or shell bras—and they most definitely do not wear plastic flowers! While dressing like a mermaid can be fun around Halloween, you can never become a mermaid or water fae, any more than they can become human. We have different natures and we must honor both.

You may be able to work with these spirits, however, or even take one as a spirit lover or companion. Always remember as you do that there are benevolent water fae and there are some that will just straight-up try to hurt you. Just like other spirits and faery folk, the finfolk have a wide variety of vibrational levels and can choose to help or to harm. In fact, some are always dangerous, some are always benevolent, and some can be both, depending on the day. So you must always be careful not to offend these watery folk.

TALES FROM THE WATERY WORLD

Below is a brief introduction to the wide variety of water fae, deities, water horses, and merfolk who populate folktales of the watery world. Later you will learn ways to work with them and connect with them through the classic mirror-and-comb technique, at the shore, or in more modern techniques of meditation and sacred bathing.

- *MacMhannain's Mermaid of Skye:* This mermaid from the Isle of Skye was once caught by a man and kept in a pool for twelve months. She is said to have shared strange secrets with him.

- *The Mermaid of Eilein Anabaich:* This wish-granting mermaid was caught by a villager on a mermaid rock. She granted him three wishes in exchange for her freedom. The man wished to be a skillful herb doctor, to have the gift of prophecy, and to have a beautiful voice. The first two wishes were granted. As to the third, although he believed he had a beautiful voice, others did not agree.

- *Liban the Mermaid:* In Celtic mythology, Liban is the beautiful sister of the Sidhe faery queen and the sea goddess Fand. Liban and her sister Fand took the form of sea birds and were struck down by the hero Cuchulainn. In revenge, the sisters found Cuchulainn as he slept and afflicted him with a strange illness that no doctor could cure. In Irish mythology, Liban and her pet dog were swept away in a great flood and found shelter in an underwater cave. She saw fish swimming by and prayed to become a salmon so that she could swim away as well. Her prayer was granted and she was turned into a mermaid—half salmon and half human. She roamed the seas with her dog for 300 years until, one day, she was caught in a net by a holy man. She was given the choice to live for 300 more years or to ascend straight to heaven. Legend says she chose the latter.

- *The Mermaid of Zennor:* This legend comes from the mid- to late-1800s. Carved benches and motifs in the local parish church in Cornwall depict a mermaid with two tails and another with a mirror and comb. It is interesting to note that the bench itself was carved sometime in the 1500s, so it is possible that the story comes from an earlier time, but was only documented much later. So what was a mermaid doing on a bench in a Cornish church in the 1500s? Legend claims that, one day, a mermaid heard the bells of the small church ringing and singing emanating from its doors. She was so enthralled by the music that she snuck up closer to hear. One young man, named Matthew, had such a beautiful voice that she promptly fell in love with him. Matthew willingly followed the mermaid down to the ocean, where they disappeared into the waves never to be seen again. Many years later, a sea captain came across the mermaid, who told him that she still lived beneath the waves with Matthew and their children. It is quite possible that she is the Saint Senara who is venerated in the same village.

- *The Old Man of Cury and the Mermaid:* An elderly man was once walking among the coves of the Lizard Peninsula, perhaps in a meditative state brought on by the liminal nature of the place. While he was walking, he saw a beautiful sea maiden who had become stranded during the change of tide. She begged the old man to carry her back to the sea and promised that, if he did, she would grant him three wishes. The old man picked her up and placed her on his shoulders. As he walked to the sea, he asked for the power to break the spells of witchcraft, the power to charm away disease, and the power to uncover stolen goods and thieves. She promised the man each of these, but told him that he must return to her on a specific day and tide, when she would meet him and instruct him in the ways of wizards. She then gave him a comb from her hair (this may have been a shell, a carved comb, or a saw-fish snout) and instructed him to call her by combing the waters.

- *The Selkie Bride:* There was once a man named Neil Mac Coddrum who was riding along the coast when he spotted a group of beautiful nude women. While enjoying the view, he stepped upon a branch, making the women aware of his presence. They ran to a pile of fur cloaks, pulled them on, and dove into the sea. Neil was able to capture the last of them, however, by retrieving her pelt before she could put it on. Thus captured, she had to live with him and become his wife. She bore him a son and daughter, both with webbed feet and fingers. They lived quietly along the shore until, one day, the children brought their selkie mother a pelt they had found. She knew immediately that it was hers. Telling her children she had to leave, she donned it and dove into the sea. Her husband was saddened, but her children could still hear her singing on some nights, beckoning them to join her in the waves.

- *The Roane:* While most selkie stories are about women, this one tells of a roane, or male selkie. A seal trapper who was out trapping and skinning seals was about to kill one when he lost his knife in the waves. The seal was able to get away. Later that night, there was a knock upon his door. When the trapper answered, he found another man who told him where he could find many seals, but said that he must go there with him. When they arrived at the spot, they were both transformed into seals and dove into the sea. They swam to where the wounded seal lay and there found the trapper's knife. He was instructed to heal the seal's wound by drawing a circle around it and placing its flipper over it. Once the seal was healed, the trapper vowed never to harm or hunt seals again.

SPIRITS OF THE MERFOLK

Tales involving merfolk are legion, and are found in almost all cultures. Some of them—like Melusine, Cerridwen, and Morgan Le Fay—we have already met. Below is a selection of other water spirits commonly found in the lore.

- *Asrai or Ashray*: Scottish water maidens whose descriptions vary from small and short to tall and thin. Sometimes they are described as ghost-like and translucent. They can only live in the water and never set foot on land. They are nocturnal and are said to turn into a puddle in sunlight.

- *Blue Men of Minch*: sea creatures that dwell in underwater caves in the Minch channel, a strait off the coast of Scotland. They are described as creatures that take the form of a man, but have blue-colored skin. They were often spotted swimming alongside boats, and were credited with luring sailors into the water and stirring up storms to wreck ships and fishing boats. They often tested a captain to see if he could save his ship by solving riddles and rhymes. In some descriptions, they are more gray than blue, and in some cases they are portrayed with wings.

- *Lir, Llyr, and Manannán mac Lir*: Irish and Welsh gods of the sea. It is possible that they are the same deity, with just slight variations in spelling and slightly different lore. Lir is known as the personification of the sea, while Manannán mac Lir is the son of the sea and is considered a psychopomp. Thus he is associated with the thinning of the veil between worlds, as well as the Celtic Otherworld. He possessed several magical items—a powerful sword named Fragarach (Answer), a cloak of invisibility (or cloak of mists), a magical cup that broke when three lies were told, and a flaming helmet. He also had a magical bag made of crane's skin that was bottomless and contained a shirt, a knife, a smith's hook, a belt of Goibniou, shears of the king of Scotland, the helmet of King Lochlann, a belt of fish skin, and the bones of a pig. He is said to have tempted the Irish King Cormac mac Airt with a silver bough containing nine apples. Some believe that the Isle of Man was named after him and that he is connected with the Welsh figure Manawydan fab Llyr.

- *Merros:* also called Moruadh or Murúghac in Gaelic. These are wild spirits that are seen off the coast by fishermen. Their presence often indicates that strong winds are coming. The females are usually described as beautiful, but have also been seen in the shape of a hornless cow, or covered in scales with a red cap. The males have green teeth and hair, and a pig's nose.

- *Nechtan:* a Celtic god of wisdom. His wife (or daughter, depending on the story) is Boann (see chapter 2); thus he is associated with the River Boyne. He was said to have three cup bearers who helped him tend the well of wisdom, which was surrounded by nine hazel trees. The nuts from the trees, when dropped into the well, granted wisdom to those who ingested them.

- *Nodens:* a Celtic god also recognized by the Gauls and associated with the sea, hunting, and dogs. He was worshipped in a temple complex found in Glouchestershire. The Romans associated him with Mars, and he is connected to the Irish Nuada and the Welsh Nudd, who was the son of Beli Mar and the father of Gwyn ap Nudd.

- *Selkies:* the seal people known to those of the British isles as half-seal, half-human creatures. They are described as very beautiful and are often depicted with dark brown hair and eyes. They are said to be able to take off their pelts, transform into humans, and walk along the shores. Legends report they, like other faery women, they can mate with men and bear human children. They are most often found in the Orkney Islands, but are well known in all of Scotland.

- *Shellycoat:* a water spirit that falls under the clas-sification of Urisk (see below), but Walter Scott described him as a type of bogle. He is found on the east coast of Scotland and described as the spirit of an eccentric man who is covered in shells and other marine life. He is usually referred to as male, and is often seen on the seashore or creating mischief in a river bed. He has been spotted in both Leith and Ettrick in Scotland, but is found elsewhere on the east coast of Britain as well. One report tells of a particularly mischievous spirit who chased travelers near the mouth of a river. He was also said to haunt the Old House of Gorrinberry on the River Hermitage in Liddesdale. When he walks, the shells that cover him clatter together, making a noise that announces his presence. On the shore of Leith, young boys ran around the spirit or the stone on which he resided three times chanting:

Shelly-coat, Shelly-coat,
Go away home;
I tremble not your mercy,
I fear not your name.

- *Shony*: a sea god worshipped in the mid-1800s by the people of Lewis. On the night of a hallow tide, a cup or chalice of ale was thrown into the sea as an offering to guarantee a good sea harvest. Alternatively, on Bride's Day, the first day of the Gaelic spring, offerings were made to earth and sea. Milk was poured on the ground, and the fisher people made porridge and threw it into the sea to ensure a bountiful catch and a good harvest of seaweed for fertilizing the soil. These practices may still continue on the island.

- *Saint Senara*: a princess of Breton who was originally named Asenora. She was described as having a "dubious reputation," but later converted to Christianity. She married a Breton king who falsely accused her of having an affair. As punishment, the king threw her into the sea trapped in a barrel and pregnant. She was visited by an angel and gave birth to a son while riding the waves; he later became Saint Budoc. She was then washed up on the coast of Cornwall and it is believed that the village there was named after her. Her story is very similar to that of Danae and Perseus. She is venerated by the local fisherman, but during medieval times, she was seen as a symbol of lust and "sins of the flesh."

In addition to these, there are many other finfolk who appear in tales and legends. Some of them—like Jenny Green Teeth, the korrigan, the cailleach, kelpies, and the Gwragedd Annwn—we have already met, along with water bulls, faery cows, and water horses. Some others include:

- *Adsullata:* a goddess of sacred springs associated with the River Savus, and sometimes associated with Sulis.

- *Aonbarr:* Manannan's magical horse of the sea, who was considered to be a helpful and benevolent water horse.

- *Argante:* one of the Arthurian Lake Ladies.

- *Aughisky:* a vicious Scottish water horse.

- *Barinthus:* the boat man who ferried King Arthur to Avalon.

- *Ben-Varrey:* mermaid-like creatures who lure men to their deaths around the Isle of Man.

- *Borvo and Bormana:* Celtic deities worshipped in France and associated with spring water.

- *Brianniul:* a sea deity similar to Shoney.

- *Brighid or Brigid:* an Irish deity, later turned saint. Like Sulis, she is associated with fire and flames, as well as with springs and holy wells. A healing goddess sometimes associated with cows, herbs, and birth, she surfaced later in Glastonbury in her saintly form.

- *Brigantia:* a goddess associated with the Braint, or Brent, River, also called Brechin and Bregenz. She may be connected to Brighid.

- *Bucca Gwidden:* water fae from Cornwall originally considered a god whose name means "white spirits."

- *Cabyll-Ushtey:* a malevolent and dangerous water horse from Scotland who eats humans or horses, usually leaving only their livers.

- *Ceasg:* a type of mermaid found in Scotland that has the tail of a salmon rather than the classic mer tail. They are often considered dangerous.

- *Cliodhna:* an Irish Queen of the Banshee who was lured back to the Otherworld by a wave called up by Manannan. The third wave in a series is sometimes called a "cliodhna wave."

- *Clota:* Welsh goddess of the River Clyde.

- *Condatis:* god of the River Wear, located in County Durham; also associated with healing in Gaul.

- *Damona:* the consort of Apollo Borvo and Apollo Moritasgus who was worshipped by both the Gauls and the Romans. Her name may be associated with the Divine Cow.

- *Deva:* goddess of the River Dee.

- *Dian Cecht:* an Irish god of healing associated with the healing spring or well called Slane near Magh Tuireadh, and also associated with the River Barrow.

- *Domnu:* a goddess of Fomoria, a bountiful land inhabited by malformed giants. She is associated with the deep primordial energies of water and wisdom, and was similar to Danu.

- *Dylan Eil Ton:* Welsh sea god whose name means "dark son of the wave." He was the son of Arianrhod and Gwydion, and twin brother to Lleu Llaw Gyffes.

- *Each-Uisge:* a Scottish water horse that lives in the lochs.

- *Fee des Houles:* sea fae that live in caves in Brittany.

- *Fiachra:* Irish King of the western sea fae.

- *Gioga:* Scottish queen of the sea trolls.

- *Glaistig Uaine:* a Scottish water imp who wears a green dress with a hood pulled down. Her skin is gray and her hair yellow, and she is sometimes depicted as half goat, half woman. She haunts rivers, lochs, lakes, and ponds. In some accounts, she is considered an intermediary between humans and faery; in others, she plays a role similar to that of Bean-Sidhe.

- *Grannus:* a Celtic sun deity associated with mineral and thermal springs.

- *Groach Vor:* a type of mermaid found in Brittany.

- *Gwenhidwy:* a Welsh shepherdess and mermaid of the nine waves. The first eight foamy waves are her sheep, the ninth her ram.

- *Gwrach y Rhibyn:* a hag-like figure with withered limbs, black talons and teeth, and large bat-like wings.

- *Gwyn ap Nudd:* faery king and ruler of Annwn who lives beneath Glastonbury Tor and guards the White Spring.

- *Haaf-fish:* a type of selkie found in the Orkney Islands.

- *Hakenmann:* a monster who lived off the north coast of Germany and had the body of a fish and the head of a man.

- *Kelpie:* a Scottish water horse often referred to as a "treacherous water devil"; a riderless horse that haunts Loch Lochy and Caledonian Canal. If you mount a kelpie, it dives deep into the cold waters and you cannot get off, so you drown in the depths.

- *Luchorpán:* Irish water leprechauns.

- *Luxivuys:* god of a thermal spring in Luxeuil, France, who was worshipped by the Gauls and Romans.

- *Mal-de-mer:* a type of sea fae found in Cornwall that cause shipwrecks and collect the souls of those who have drowned.

- *Mara-Warra:* Irish mermaids who have many riches and many underworld dwellings.

- *Mari Morgan:* a Celtic mer fae found in the British Isles.

- *Mary Player:* English mermaid who sank ships by swimming three times around them.

- *Matrona:* a mother goddess associated with the River Marne.

- *Morgawr:* a giant sea serpent that is often found lurking in the waters of Falmouth Bay.

- *Muireartach:* a Scottish sea serpent or sea fae that appears as an old woman with one eye.

- *Murdhuachas:* Irish sea fae with the head of a seal.

- *Nehalennia:* Germanic or Celtic goddess associated with the Rhine River and the North Sea. She is depicted with marine motifs, dogs, and ships.

- *Niamh:* the daughter of Mannan Mac Lir whose name means "Bright One" or "Radiant One." She is said to have crossed the sea on a magical horse.

- *Nix or Nixie:* German water spirits who were shapeshifters and often appeared in many different forms. "Nixie" denotes the female; "Nix" denotes the male. They were also called Neck or Nokken, and the females are often called River Maids. They take various forms and sometimes resemble kelpies or water horses.

- *Nuggle:* a type of water horse from the Shetland Islands.

- *Sea Mither* **or** *Mither of the Sea:* a Scottish water spirit deriving from Orkney who rides a malelovent water horse to the depths of the ocean and battles with her enemy, Teran, every year. *Mither* is a Scots variant of the word "mother."

- *Sea trows:* selkie-like creatures who are connected with the weather. If one is killed or wounded, a great storm may come. In Shetland, this is the name for mermaids.

- *Sequana:* a Gaulish river deity who dwells in the River Seine in France. She was particularly associated with the spring that feeds the river, where a healing shrine was found that dates back to the first century BCE.

- *Shoopiltees:* a water pony from Orkney.

- *Sinann:* an Irish goddess of the River Shannon, also called Siannan.

- *Souconna:* goddess of the River Seine in France.

- *Tangie:* a mischievous Scottish water horse.

- *Tarroo-Ushtey:* a water bull from the Isle of Man that is considered dangerous.

- *Tegid Foel:* a Welsh deity, Cerridwen's husband, who is associated with Lake Bala (Llyn Tegid).

- *The White Lady:* a faery-like spirit often seen near rivers, canals, and springs.

- *Uilebheist:* a Gaelic multiheaded sea monster found near Scotland.

- *Urisk of Ben Doran:* a wild-man type spirit associated with a waterfall at Ben Doran.

- *Verbeia:* a British/Roman goddess of the River Wharfe whose single shrine stands in Ilkley.

- *Wachilt:* a sea goddess recognized by both Celtic and Germanic peoples. She was said to be a wild goddess who halted ships. She was also described as a sea witch or giantess, and as the mother of the legendary master blacksmith, Wayland Smith.

WATER ANIMALS

The waters of the earth are home to myriad species, some of whom play a significant role in water magic. Some of them—like dolphins, frogs, and lobsters—we have already met. Here are some others whose powers you can use in your workings:

- *Crabs:* These crustaceans are associated with the zodiac sign of Cancer, a cardinal water sign. They come in many varieties, from the velvet crab, to the spider crab, to hermit crabs, to the crabs we commonly see with large pincers. Crab claws are used magically for protection. Hermit crab shells that have been shed can be exceptional tools for protection and invisibility. Crabs help us manage our emotions and attitudes because they are strongly associated with the moon and the ocean, and carry these energies as well. They can be used in spells concerning growth, rebirth, protection, shielding, clarity, retreat, cycles, vision, sensitivity, and hurt feelings.

- *Gulls:* Gulls are associated with communication, expression, responsibility, diet, and stimuli. Because these birds are so closely related to beaches and have a tendency to clean beaches by ingesting and removing debris, they can be powerful allies in beach-cleaning endeavors. Because our waters and beaches have become so polluted, however, they often die from ingesting plastic and other toxic substances. In Wales, it was believed that sea gulls could help foretell the weather.

- *Herons and egrets:* These majestic, beautiful, and kind creatures are my favorite birds. They walk between the worlds, able to navigate through air, mud, and water. They live off small fish in the oceans and marshes. They remind us to stand tall and proud, and to stand up for what we believe. They are often seen at dusk and dawn. For this reason, as well as for their ability to live in varied elements, I consider them to be great allies for hedge riders. They can be used in magic regarding balance, progression, evolution, following your own path, wisdom, intuition, determination, pursuit of opportunity, grounding, stability, and liminality. They also bring the worlds together and are a symbol of balance.

- *Otters:* Playfulness, happiness, curiosity, awakening, pleasure, and imagination are the characteristics of this small water creature. They tend to be very motherly and navigate the waters with ease and gracefulness. If you ever have a chance to watch them, you will see that they are amazing creatures who slide, spin, and glide through the waters.

- *Salmon:* This fascinating fish was considered very sacred by many cultures and represents the cycle of death and rebirth. The salmon is a very strong and resilient creature that swims upstream to spawn, then returns downstream. When the young are grown and ready to spawn themselves, they fight their way upstream to the place where they began, often scaling white rapids and flinging themselves over banks to perpetuate the cycle of death and rebirth. In Celtic lore, the salmon appears in stories about Cerridwen and in the story of the fisher king, where it represents wisdom and is intimately connected with the hazel nut. Salmon can be used in magic concerning cycles of life and death, strength, going against the current, traveling home, and wisdom.

- *Seahorses:* These are amazing creatures that burst forth by the hundreds from a seahorse pouch after being incubated by the male of the species. They are very "otherworldly" in both their shape and in the way they move. In some places, seahorses are considered talismans of protection and they are often dried and hung in the home or carried about. In some cases, small beads made of glass, particularly blue beads, are added to the talisman to avert the evil eye and strengthen the charm.

- *Swan:* You are probably very familiar with swans from the story of the ugly duckling. Swans are all about transformation—transforming from the "ugly duck" into one of the most beautiful birds. The Celts believed that the swan was associated with the sun and "a new dawn," but they also believed that souls often took the shape of a swan when traveling to the Underworld, thus continuing the theme of evolution or shapeshifting. Swans are liminal creatures that can transport magical folk to other realms—often the subaqueous realms.

Others water animals and their associations include:

- *Cuttlefish:* masters of disguise, shapeshifting, transformation, and hiding

Mermaids and Finfolk

- *Dragonflies:* transformation, new perspectives, and metamorphosis

- *Ducks:* self-nurturing, comfort, grace, and floating on calm or rough waters

- *Eels:* shapeshifting, transformation, male sexuality, defense, battle, warrior, and thunder

- *Jellyfish:* protection, buoyancy, and transparency

- *Octopus:* escape from tight situations, protection, quick thinking, and blending in with your surroundings

- *Seals:* balance, dreamtime, creative force, focus, and the imagination

- *Sharks:* development of the senses, journeys, exploration of the deep, fearlessness, authority, power, and protection

- *Starfish:* resilience, regeneration, and perseverance

- *Turtles:* longevity, awakening, blessings, taking the slow road, shielding, protection, and new perspectives

- *Water serpents:* rebirth, resurrection, wisdom, healing, alchemy, and shedding of old habits

- *Whales:* ancient symbol for creation, aid in shielding, containment, concealment, deep creative inspira-

tion, nurturing, taking the slow road, and feelings
and situations that are larger than life

MIRROR AND COMB MAGIC

Across the globe, from Europe to Africa and from Japan
to South America, mermaids have been depicted holding combs and mirrors. In the story of the mermaid and
the old man of Cury, we see that a comb can be used
to summon a mermaid if properly enchanted. Cecil
Williamson, founder of the Museum of Witchcraft and
Magic, suggests that mermaid combs used in Britain were
actually the snouts of saw fish. They were used to rake
patterns into the sand to prepare sacred spaces in which
bones could be cast. While many sources associate mermaids' mirrors with vanity, I suggest that their mirrors
and combs had a more magical purpose. The combs were
used as magical tools to summon spirits, while the mirrors—and by extension, the glassy surfaces of lakes and
wells—became symbols of the Otherworld and acted as
portals.

We know that mirrors can act as portals—
witness Alice, who enters Wonderland through a mirror
in *Through the Looking Glass*. I also find it interesting that
both red and white roses appear as symbols throughout
both of Carroll's books, as these are colors of the Celtic
Otherworld and of Avalon. Lewis Carroll was strongly
influenced by Masonic traditions, which have ties to

the Golden Dawn and similar magical fraternities. He may thus have used these colors and symbols deliberately, although we can never know for sure. Nonetheless, Alice's adventures show us that mirrors can connect us to other realms. And they can also connect us to the ocean and to perfectly still lakes reflecting the Full Moon.

It is curious as well that there are many effigies, carvings, and reliefs of mermaids that adorn churches across Europe, as seen in the one found in Zennor (see above). It is widely believed that these decorations are remnants from Pagan times, when wells, rivers, and groves were sacred to the local spirits. Later, when Christians began to build churches over these sites, the mer form was used to honor the spirit of the place and the local beliefs in an attempt to gain converts. Mirrors and combs are often included in these decorations.

Exercise: Enchanting a Mirror

Enchanting a mirror to be used as a portal or a viewing tool can be very effective. You do this by charging the mirror with intent. First, however, you must cleanse and consecrate the mirror with holy water or spring water. Once that is done, you can charge it with your intent to make it a portal. If you are not comfortable working with or entering a portal, you can charge the mirror as a remote viewing tool and use it as you would a crystal ball or bowl of water for scrying. You can also use a mirror as a means to work with a particular spirit.

Practice opening and closing your mirror portal by drawing pentagrams over it with your finger. It is important that you use both opening and closing pentagrams when you work with a portal. Open the portal by drawing an opening pentagram on its surface using holy water. Close the portal by drawing a closing or banishing pentagram. I will not give you specific instructions for drawing each pentagram, as many traditions draw them differently. Just stay with your own path or tradition and draw these as you usually would.

Keep a black cloth on hand to wrap the mirror when it is not in use. Always use caution when working with portals, and be sure to cleanse well after your work.

Exercise: Combing the Water

Find a comb that you want to work with magically. Cleanse it in any way you choose that maintains a watery, sea, or mermaid theme. Then consecrate it using rose water or some other beautiful scent. If you choose to work with an antique comb, be sure to cleanse it well first.

When your comb is ready, take it to the water. This ritual works best at the seashore, but, as you have seen, water spirits are everywhere and many mermaids have been reported to live in lakes as well. Just be sure to choose a place where you are comfortable and where you can walk to the water easily. Sit by whatever body of water you have chosen and put yourself into an altered state of consciousness. A light meditative state will work, as will a deep trance-like state.

Begin to comb the water, singing or chanting softly. You can use your own chant or song, or you can use something like this:

Mermaids of the sea,
For so long you've hidden from me;
Mermaids of the tide,
Come to me, no longer hide;
Merfolk of the ocean,
Delicate waves caressing,
Grant me this blessing.

Comb the water and sing until you feel you have fin-ished. Then return to where you were sitting and bring yourself into a deeper altered state of consciousness. Open your mind to the possibilities of mermaids, seeing them in both this realm and the Otherworld. Spend time just resting in the possibility of mermaids. If you happen to see mermaids in either realm, keep a safe distance and just observe. Watch their movements; notice the way they look and how they interact with the environment. If they notice you, keep your interactions very basic and polite.

Caution: Never go into the ocean with merfolk, even if you want to! Merfolk and other water spirits have a bad habit of drowning those who offend them. Be sure that you remain on the shore at a safe distance so you cannot be swept out to sea.

Exercise: Dark Moon Mermaid Bath

In this exercise, you will begin to work with the energies of the merfolk and of the sea. This bath is best taken during the Dark Moon. Because mermaids are mysterious, live in the depths of the sea, and most likely live beyond the veil, Dark Moon energies can draw us closest to them. Be sure to charge your bath ingredients with the intent to connect to mermaid energy before you get into the tub, and remember to bring your comb along with you for this bath.

Combine the following ingredients in a cup or bowl and charge them with your intent:

- Rosemary

- Equal parts of Epsom and sea salt

- Baking soda

- Kelp

- Bladderwrack

- Nine drops sea water

Cleanse and consecrate your space, and use black candles if you choose to light them. Begin to fill the tub with water and pour your charged mixture into the tub. Take your comb and comb the water as in the previous exercise, singing and chanting as you do. When you feel mer and ocean energies present, climb in and soak in the bath.

In your mind's eye, or using a mirror to scry, begin summoning the merfolk with your song. If any merfolk appear, spend time in meditation and talk to them. Be sure to ask if they have come in good will. If they have, continue to speak with them. If they haven't, be sure to thank them for visiting and tell them that you want nothing from them and wish them well. If you are unsure of their intentions, try asking them three times in a row. Lore tells us that spirits can't lie three times in a row.

Ask the merfolk what you may call them, and if you may share that name with others. Ask them how they want your relationship with them to work. Are they interested in having a human companion, or do they dislike human nature? Are they amenable to your summoning them for help in the future? Ask them anything you like, but be sure not to ask for favors or gifts the first few times you contact them. These are very selfish acts and the merfolk are easily offended. If they give you a gift, that is great! If not, be sure that they know you are there only to speak to them and nothing more. When you are finished, acknowledge their gift and their time. Be sure to ask if you may visit again and if they would like you to bring anything with you. Be sure to visit soon so you can build your relationship with them.

Chapter 9

Water Witchery

In this chapter, we will explore how to create potions and use them in water magic. There are many ways to work with potions. Some believe that tea, coffee, juice, and other beverages can even be used in magical potions, while others believe potions can only be distilled using precise techniques that employ science and astrology. I suggest creating potions by combining different ingredients in a water base following one of two methods. Hopefully, you will begin to use these methods to make your own potions for use in your own practice.

Both of these methods start with a water base. You can choose just about any kind of water for this base, depending on your need. If you are going to ingest the potion, be sure to use drinkable water. If you are not, you can use snow, ice, rain water, river water, ocean water, or any other kind of water. Be sure that you label everything carefully. Note those potions that are drinkable and those that are not, list the ingredients, and include the date and any astrological information that is pertinent. If you are like me, you will most likely make more than you need to use at any one time. I actually recommend doing this, because it is handy to have an arsenal of potions ready for use so you will use them often. Don't make potions and then let them sit on the shelf and get dusty, however. Get out there and work your magic! You can carry a vial or two on your person and use them in magical workings wherever you go. Or you can use them in daily devotional rites, in simple spell work, or as gifts to other magical friends.

The first method I recommend is called the "mother method," which involves making several large batches of single-ingredient bases. For example, you may use several different types of holy water and many different tinctures, hydrosols, and gemstone elixirs to make mixtures that are each charged with a specific and singular purpose. These can then be combined to make more complicated and very targeted potions. Take a bowl, cauldron, or jar and fill it about three quarters full with the base water; then begin to add your tinctures and elixirs. You can choose to add nine drops of each, or use a number that aligns with your work. The benefit of this method is that you have instant access to your potion and don't have to wait six to nine weeks for tinctures to mature, or twenty-four hours for flower waters to steep.

The second method involves combining all your ingredients into a watery or alcohol base and letting it sit for however long it needs to, depending on your ingredients. For example, you can add mugwort, lapis, and some brandy to rose water and let it sit for six weeks before using it. The benefit to this method is that you create a unique potion charged with a specific purpose. The downside is that, if you don't use enough alcohol, the potion can spoil. I have experienced potions that just did *not* turn out well. This can be a learning experience, however, and failing at a particular potion can also be a way of ruling out a specific formula. The only way to learn how to create powerful potions for your magic is to get in there and start using them. Some may turn out amazingly well, and you will want to record them in your journal. Others may turn out to be weak, or unreliable, or flat-out moldy. But remember: Sometimes that mold may be just what you need—after all, it is watery mold!

Each of these methods will create a useful potion. Use the formulas below to get some experience in making potions. Later, you can begin creating custom blends. You will see some very loose formulas below, and they are this way for a reason. In the following formulas, I give you measurements by "parts." When you measure things by parts—for example, 1 part herb and 2 parts resin— you can easily convert the measurement to something more precise—for example, 1 ounces herb and 2 ounces resin, or 1 cup herb and 2 cups resin.

I call my own method for creating blends the "Wise Woman" method. This method involves using your intuition. Leave the measuring spoons behind and create your blends following your instinct. Water is the element of intuition after all! On the other hand, it is always good to triple check yourself against academic resources.

Caution: Know your plants, stones, oils, and ingredients before ingesting anything. You are responsible for what you put into your body. Be sure to consult a doctor before using any herb.

SACRED FLOWER WATER

There are two ways to use flowers and water. The first is to make water for rituals using flowers; the other is to make your own flower essences.

Flower water is water into which you have put flowers and let steep—usually for about twenty-four hours, but not more. It is preserved with alcohol and is highly concentrated. The water is then strained and treated using a variety of methods, including sun infusion and moon infusion. You can even add quartz to the water to amp up its power. I make my flower waters using a number of flowers all together—for instance, combining rose petals, pansy, and calendula. But you can also make them each individually and then combine them in ritual or spell work using a dropper. The water will take on the energy and intent of the flowers used. You can use flower waters in your baths, rituals, and spells.

Flower essences are liquid extracts that are ingested to address issues of emotional well-being, soul development, and mind-body health. They are usually made as a water-and-sun infusion using wild flowers, garden flowers, or organically grown pesticide-free store-bought flowers, then bottled individually.

The most important thing to remember when creating flower waters and flower essences is: *Know your flowers*. It is your responsibility to know what you are using, whether it is safe to ingest, or how it can be used safely in magic. If you are unsure, use roses, as they are easy to get and are safe.

You can preserve any of these blends with a little brandy or vodka. If you prefer your water to be alcohol-free, you can freeze it until you need it. If you do choose to freeze it, make sure you use a container that can expand. In this case, unfortunately, you may have to use plastic.

Exercise: Making Flower Water

Purchase distilled water, or make your own if you can. Choose a sacred vessel or a good clean bowl and fill it one half to three quarters full with water. Place your flowers in the bowl so they float on the water. Set the bowl out in the sun and let it sit for one to two hours.

Remove the flowers and strain the water if necessary; then place the water in a jar with a lid. Depending on how much you have made, add about one eighth that amount of brandy or vodka to preserve it. For example, if you made 1 cup of infusion, add 1/8 cup of brandy.

GEMSTONE ELIXIRS

Making elixirs with gemstones is simple and fun, but there are some basic things you must keep in mind. Not every stone is safe to use; some stones are water soluble, while others are downright toxic. Because of this, we will talk here about two different methods for making sacred elixirs using gemstones: the direct and the indirect. The first infuses the stone directly into the water; the second creates a protective barrier between the stone and the water. This is the method that must be used with toxic stones.

Caution: Do not drink any water that has been directly infused with toxic stones. *Do your research.* A general rule is that anything in the agate or quartz family is usually safe to ingest. For any other stone—research! If you can't find any information on the stone you want to use, it is better to be safe than sorry and use the indirect method. You can also use rose waters, moon or sun water, and even tea. In fact, you can actually create your elixirs using any previously prepared or collected waters.

Exercise: Making Direct Gemstone Elixirs

Take your favorite water and place it in a clean glass or jar. Charge your stone with your intent and drop it in the water. Cover the container if you need to and let it sit overnight. The next morning, bottle up the elixir and save it. In the future, you can charge it with moonlight or sunlight.

Exercise: Making Indirect Gemstone Elixirs

First, choose your stone. You will also need two bowls—one small and one large—and either distilled or filtered water. Place the small bowl inside the large bowl. Then set the stone inside the small bowl. Pour the distilled or filtered water into the large bowl, making sure the water does not flow over into the smaller bowl. Let this sit overnight. Then remove the small bowl containing the stone. Bottle up the water that is left in the large bowl and label it properly, including the date, the name of the stone, and any other ingredients you used. This water will be drinkable, as long as you have made sure that the water did not touch the stone.

USING MAGIC POTIONS AND ELIXIRS

Potions and elixirs made using the methods given above, and many others, can be used in all kinds of magical workings. Here are just a few examples.

Healing Potion

This potion can be used to anoint candles, sprinkle on an altar, or for any healing magic. To create it, you will need:

- 1 part blue calcite elixir
- 1 part blue-lace agate elixir
- 1 part speedwell herbal water
- 1 part yarrow flower essence

Combine these ingredients and add them to a spray bottle or a sacred vessel during healing rites. You can also anoint yourself and objects with this potion.

Love Potion

Who doesn't love a good old-fashioned love potion? This potion will not bring you a specific lover. Instead, it is used in sex magic and general love rituals, and is essentially an aphrodisiac. To create this potion, you will need:

- 1 cup brandy
- 1 pinch wormwood
- 9 apple blossoms
- 3 pinches red rose petals

Combine the plant ingredients in a jar and pour in the brandy, making sure to cover all the other ingredients with the brandy. Let the mixture sit for nine weeks; then strain and bottle it. Please note that this potion does not have a water base, but several drops of it can be added to a bath or glass of wine (wink).

Triple Moon Elixir

This elixir is both not what it seems and exactly what it says! This is a watery potion that you can bottle or use as a spray. It combines three potent moon symbols—a moonstone, a white rose, and a pearl—with a base of silvered water. While it is meant to be a potent moon potion, it also resonates with the Wiccan Triple Goddess. Just drop the moon symbols in the silvered water and charge the elixir under the light of the moon.

Seasonal Potions

Many potions are used as a part of magical workings at specific times of the year or during specific phases of the moon. These are not meant to be ingested; rather they are to be used in bath preperations or to wash floors, anoint candles, as ritual waters, and to work spells. You can also use them in sprays, offering bowls, and floor or hair washes. While water is not listed in every recipe below use it as the main base unless a specific type is suggested

- *Yule:* Combine cedar, fir, and wintergreen in a snow or ice base. Use immediately or preserve with alcohol. (Not to be ingested)

- *Imbolc:* Prepare a bowl of snow base. Float a candle on top of it and light it. Let the candle burn down as the snow melts. If you don't have access to snow, use spring water and add crushed ice. Sprinkle the water with rowan and cowslip (*Primula veris*) and let it sit during Imbolc. Then bottle it and preserve, or give it as an offering to the land by pouring it onto the ground.

- *Spring equinox:* Combine rose petals, quartz elixir, primrose, saffron (crocus), scotch broom, and columbine in a rose-water base. Other flower essences

work well too. Strain the petals, or leave them in—
your choice!

- *Beltaine:* Combine hawthorn flowers, hawthorn
  leaves, rose blooms, blue bells, yarrow, and red-
  jasper elixir.

- *Summer solstice:* Combine thistle, coltsfoot, dandelion, heather, citrine elixir, yellow calcite elixir, and
  carnelian elixir.

- *Lammas/First Harvest:* Combine sun-shower water base
  with nine drops of (clean) lake water and add honey
  and Oat Straw.

- *Fall equinox:* Combine orange calcite elixir, three
  beautifully colored fall leaves, blackberry leaves,
  nine rose hips, and three hawthorn haws.

- *Samhain:* On the stove, combine rose, rosemary, lavender, and lemon balm with 3/4 cup of your favorite
  Merlot. Simmer for just a few minutes; then let cool
  and strain so that only the liquid remains. Pour the
  warm liquid into a large juice container and add
  the juice of a pomegranate and the juice of 1 cup
  of blackberries. Pour the remainder of the bottle of
  Merlot into the container. Cover, chill, and don't
  forget you can use this for more than just a delicious
  drink!

- *Eclipse:* Combine sun water, Dark Moon water, quartz (or moonstone), sunstone, and black moonstone or onyx in a bowl and set it out for the duration of the eclipse.

Unity Water

Collect these waters if you have access to them. If not, make modifications by adding salt, shells, and seaweed to distilled water.

- Rain water

- River water

- Spring or well water

- Ocean water

- Sacred holy water (either gathered from a sacred source or created with a blessing)

- Full Moon water

- Dark Moon water

Combine the waters and let them sit; then strain. This will collect the essence of all the waters and allow you to bring their combined powers to your magical workings.

WASHES AND PURIFYING SPRAYS

Water witches use washes and purifying sprays to prepare for rituals, and to ensure successful workings. Here are a few examples.

Magical Hair Washes

Magical hair washes can be used as part of a ritual bath, or to purify and cleanse before a ritual. These herbs should either be added to a bath or steeped in a bowl of water in which your hair can be washed or dipped. Alternatively, you can use this mixture as a spray.

- Combine white rose, for balance, with angelica, for cleansing.

- Combine seaweed, to connect with the sea and promote growth, with witch hazel, for hair cleansing and scalp health.

- Combine nettle, to nourish, with peppermint, to promote growth, and eyebright, to spiritually cleanse, grant wisdom, strengthen the third eye, and connect to the Otherworld.

- Combine lavender, to promote beauty, with nine drops rose oil, for health and balance.

New Moon Floor Wash

Floor washes are great for cleansing a home. I like to use mine around the spring equinox, but Samhain is also a great choice, and any other time will do as well. Use this floor wash on the New Moon.

Start by soaking your herbs in either spring water or water you have collected from a sacred source. You can also use silvered water or holy water created with a hagstone. Add:

- White rose petals to bring beauty and serenity, and to add a bit of bite from the thorns

- Heather, which is traditionally used in protection spells

- Rosemary, which is known to banish and heal, and is used in exorcism

- Vervain, which is used for purification and consecrating

- 3 drops rose oil

- 3 drops rosemary oil

- 3 drops lavender oil

Preserve the mixture with some white vinegar. The smell of all these together is just delightful! If you don't have tile or wood floors, don't worry. You can use the water in the form of a spray anywhere in the house or to complete a sweeping ritual with your broom if you have one. Make sure to leave the door open to sweep all of the past out the door!

Basic Spray Blend

If you are unable to burn incense in an apartment due to restrictions, or have asthma, or just prefer to use water-based materials, try making a spray. Sprays are really fun to make. All you need to do is gather your plant material, boil it in some water, and strain it out. Add a preservative like brandy or vodka and a few drops of an essential oil. Let the mixture cool before transferring it into a spray bottle. Here's a formula I like to use:

- 3 parts boiled plant material (strain the water)

- 1/16 part essential oils (you really only need a few drops)

- 1 part preservative (like brandy or vodka)

HEALING AND CLEANSING BATHS

Bathing rituals are often very personal and each practitioner may perform these rites differently. Below I give you bath recipes that are left intentionally general so that you can tailor them to your own path and practice.

Those who follow Neo-Pagan paths may want to take baths on the Sabbats—perhaps a warm bath filled with fresh juicy sliced apples, or a brightly lit white candle ritual for Imbolc, or a chakra-aligning bath using colored stones or flowers that correspond to the chakra system. Those who work the shadow path may want to take extra baths on the Dark Moons, and use things like black candles, rose petals, and black salts to work shadow healing magic or journey to the Underworld using the drain as a portal. They may even practice necromancy with incense and smoke of wormwood and mugwort.

For land-locked sea witches, water baths may be necessary to keep them balanced. Consider experimenting with sea salt from different regions, or even making your own. I have a very small clay jar of salt that I made myself from the sea waters of Okinawa, Japan. Although I only have a small quantity, this salt has become one of my most powerful tools. I only use a tiny pinch at a time and only when I need that extra power and personal touch.

Come up with a personal schedule or mark special days to perform these bathing rituals. Rituals of healing are very important. Water, being an element of both life and destruction, is the perfect modality for healing the wounds of the soul, and also for providing a warm comforting cocoon for meditations that can lead you to meet your shadow self. The possibilities are endless!

Amethyst Bath

For centuries, amethyst was believed to help fight addictions. The Greeks and Romans made chalices out of this stone to prevent intoxication. This stone is a powerful tool for shadow work and for dealing with the uglier sides of ourselves.

This bath is best used during the Dark Moon. Use your bath water as a vessel for making a gemstone elixir bath. On the day of the Dark Moon, ritually prepare for your bath. Spend time pondering your vices and short-comings. Place an amethyst in your bathtub, fill the tub with water, and light black candles (or dark candles) around the tub. When you are ready, step into your tub, taking care not to step or slip on the stone.

Sink into the bath and relax. Locate the amethyst and bring it to your belly or hold it in your palm. Begin to meditate on your addictions or other things you want to release. When you are done contemplating, step out of the bath, leaving as much water as you can in the tub. When you are dry, remove your stone and pull the drain plug. Visualize all the muck going down the drain and taking anything you no longer want with it. Rinse your stone in cold water (not your bath water) and set it out under the Full Moon to recharge and cleanse it.

Rose Bath

Roses come in many sizes, shapes, and colors. Some may have as few as four petals, while others possess over 100. Some are incredibly fragrant, and others are just stunningly beautiful. Whichever rose you choose, bathing in roses is simply luxurious! It is great for your skin, and for your spiritual health. The rose speaks of mystery, magic, light and dark, beauty and bane.

Gather your rose petals and fill your bathtub with water. When it is about ¼ full, begin to drop the petals into the water. When you are satisfied with how it feels, climb in and relax. Really take this time to soak and enjoy—to get to know the rose. There is much power in these beautiful blooms, and I have found that they can connect with almost any element—yellow roses with air, red roses with fire, etc. Record any messages you receive from the sweet fragrance of the roses and the water. You may find the rose to be a soft gentle teacher, like the soft and sweet petals of her bloom, or you may find it to be a more harsh mentor, like the thorns that protect its stems. Whatever side of the rose speaks to you, listen to the message transmitted through the water.

Stress-Release Gemstone Bath

For this ritual, prepare a gemstone elixir from Blue Lace Agate using the direct method. You will also be adding Epsom salts and vervain to the bath. Bring the elixir into your bath area with you, fill your tub, and set the mood with blue candles.

When your bath is ready, add vervain, either in a pouch or directly to the bath water. Then step into the water. Sit back and relax; spend time soaking in the waters. When you are ready, take your container of gemstone elixir in both hands, with the lid off. Feel all the day's stress melting right off you. When you are ready, say:

> I relax within (Take a sip)
> I relax all about (Pour a bit of elixir into the bath)
> Water in (Take a sip)
> And water out (Pour elixir into the bath)

Repeat this until all the elixir is gone. Let the stone fall into the water as well. Relax; really spend time de-stressing, letting the water do the work! When you are ready, get out of the tub, retrieve your stone, rinse it in cold water, and then grab a glass of wine!

Quartz-Crystal Bath for Healing a Wounded Ego

You can create a crystal bath by placing several crystals in the water, or by creating a crystal grid around the tub. If you don't work with crystals, or don't have any, you can also use hagstones, fossils, river rocks, or smooth stones like agate or quartz that have washed up on a beach. This bath may be done at any time and draws its power from quartz (to release memories and restore balance), rose quartz (to bring love and beauty back to your heart and soul), and smokey quartz (to help process trauma and to grant forgiveness for mistakes made). The water helps to amplify the healing properties of these stones.

Fill the tub with water and place all three stones in the water. When you are ready, get in and be careful not to step on the stones. Settle in and relax. Then begin by thinking of the situation that you are processing. Focus on it and bring it to the front of your mind. When you are ready, take the smokey quartz in your hand and meditate with it. Let its energy flow into the water and surround your body. When you are done, release the stone into the water, and do the same with the other stones. Let them teach you. Then let them fall back into the water.

When you feel the bath is finished, remove the stones and stand up. Pull the plug and use the drain exercise from chapter 2 to let the water and all negativity flow out of the tub and down the drain.

Cleansing Bath

The purpose of this ritual is to cleanse your physical and energetic bodies. When you focus your intent into the water, make sure that cleansing your physical body, your energetic body, and your spirit is foremost in your mind. Do not rush. The herbs and salts it uses are very effective at cleansing toxins from the body. So to really enjoy your bath, take your time! I recommend doing this ritual on the Full Moon, but the New Moon and waxing moon are also appropriate.

Start by having a clean bathroom. Once all is to your liking, turn on the water and begin to fill the tub. Blend vervain, white rose petals, angelica, and sea salt in a dish. When the tub is full, undress and take a handful of your mixture and visualize the moon. Then visualize your heart center. Finally, visualize water.

Visualize the water crashing over you and cleansing you. Visualize your heart center being cleansed of heavy burdens. Visualize the energy of the moon cleansing and consecrating you. Bring all these images together to form a blue ball of light or shining water in your mind's eye.

Now breathe these energies out and over the dish of herbs, charging them with your intent. When you feel they are charged, pour the herb mixture into the tub and get in. Sink down into the waters and relax; enjoy several moments (or longer) and let your body enjoy the water on your skin. Close your eyes and find a state of being where you can relax, breathe rhythmically, and open your mind to visualization.

When you are finished with your visualization, repeat the charm below three times:

Oh sacred waters I conjure thee,
Come forth and cleanse me;
Work the will for which I pray,
Eo-deo-ah-hey-yeh.

Sink into the water until it covers your head. It is also quite effective if you dip down in the water three times as you speak your charm. When you are ready, open your eyes and finish your bath however you like. When you are finished, pull the plug and let the water flow down and out the drain. Let any other unwanted energy flow out of you and down the drain with the water. This process can be repeated or used as inspiration for any of the baths below. Just substitute the ingredients and intent!

Seaweed Beauty Bath

For this bath, you will need:

- Dulce
- Bladderwrack
- Kelp
- 9 drops of dew
- 9 drops of sea water
- 9 drops of holy or sacred well water

Combine the ingredients and add to your tub.

Sea Shell Bath for Luck and Good Fortune

Shells are considered to be very lucky and can bring good fortune. Choose you favorite shell and take a bath with it! Be sure to let the shell soak in the water with you.

Evil-Eye Removal Bath

For this rite, you will need:

- 3 cowrie shells
- 3 cat's eye shells (or snail shells)
- 3 moon shells

Add all three to the bath after you are in and settled.

Protection Bath

To prepare this bath, you will need:

- Blessed thistle
- St. John's wort
- Hawthorn
- Rowan
- Yarrow
- Rosemary

Add the ingredients to your bath and soak in their protective powers.

Shapeshifting Bath

For this bath, you will need:

- Angelica
- A red rose
- A white rose
- A pearl (fresh-water pearls are a good option)
- Water from a magical, holy, or sacred spring

Prepare a bath using these ingredients and connect with Melusine.

MOON AND SEASONAL BATHS

Just as certain potions are used at certain times of the year or during certain phases of the moon, so some bathing rituals are most powerful at those times. Here are a few modern recipes that connect with the seasons and moon cycles::

- *Full Moon:* On the Full Moon, add a large white circular stone or tumbled quartz, some angelica, and some chamomile to your bath. Decorate the tub with white candles and connect to the Full Moon to make the bath more powerful.

- *Dark Moon:* Combine dark red roses, a tumbled garnet, a tumbled onyx, a tumbled smokey quartz, and onyx in your bath. You can also use black tourmaline, but you must make a gemstone elixir first, using the indirect method. Do not put it directly into the bath.

- *Samhain:* This is the Witches' Sabbat. Add three apple slices (sliced so the pentagram shows), a handful of dark-red rose petals, a garnet, and blackberry juice to your bath.

- *Winter solstice:* Combine three pinches of peppermint with some freshly fallen snow and add to your bath. You can substitute crushed ice if you live in a warm climate.

- *Imbolc:* Add Epsom salts to your tub and set white candles around it. Before you bathe, create three Brigid crosses and use them to decorate the bath.

- *Spring equinox:* Add fresh pink and white rose petals, pansy, and yarrow to your bath water.

- *Beltane:* Add hawthorn flowers (preferably fresh, but dried work nicely too), pink rose petals, and yarrow to your tub.

- *Summer solstice:* Add nine dandelion heads (dried leaves work as well), three pinches of lemon balm, nine pinches of heather, and some St. John's wort to your bath water. Note: Ingesting St. John's wort can have an effect on medication and birth control, so use caution with this bath.

- *First harvest:* Add 1 cup of milk and some honey to your bath to connect with the Lady of Llyn Y Fan Fach and her faery cow. If you are vegan, try substituting ½ cup oats. You can dedicate this bath to Brigid as well.

- *Fall equinox:* Rinse nine beautifully colored fall leaves with hot water and vinegar and place them in your bath, along with carnelian and three pinches of calendula.

OTHER RITUAL BATHS

Baths have also traditionally been used for curse removal, purification, and grounding, and for a variety of other purposes. Here are a few examples from the record.

- *Curse removal:* This bath is a bit different, as it is done at a body of water—ideally a river, but also at the ocean—and not in your own tub. Choose a location and dress yourself in white. When you arrive at your chosen spot, step into the water with your back toward the flow of the river. If you are at the ocean, let the waves crash over you or orient yourself so that the tide is flowing toward your back. I suggest only going out far enough so that the water comes to your chest while sitting. Bring a friend with you and always be careful, as river currents and ocean tides can be quite powerful.

- *Purification:* Add vervain, white rose petals, and three pinches of sea salt to your bath water, leaving the salt until last. Stir the bath sunwise three times while saying: "Three pinches of salt stirred thrice about, I hereby cast all bane out!"

- *Grounding:* Place three white stones gathered from a river and one pyritized ammonite in your bath to ground and center you. You can use this bath in preparation for a ritual, or just to bring yourself into a relaxed and grounded state.

- *Beauty:* Add nine drops of dew collected before sunrise on May 1st, some hawthorn flowers, and some yarrow to your tub.

Conclusion

The information found within these pages is a combination of historical fact, folklore, and my own experience. Water magic and Celtic culture have both long been obsessions of mine. During my many years of practice and research, I have rediscovered many traditions that had been lost to the past and were absent from most modern books on witchcraft. Over time, the information I uncovered began to merge with my own magical practice and this led me to consider that there was, in fact, a water cult—an entire spiritual path—that had deep historical roots in Europe and in other cultures around the world. As this spiritual path became clearer to me, I realized that it was, indeed, a path rich in lore, history, and magical application. This is what led me to write this book.

I have found, however, that modern witches must make adjustments to this body of lore in order for it to be relevant to them today. Many tools, for instance, are available to witches today that were perhaps not readily available hundreds of years ago. Thus many of the old charms found in this book have been rewritten in my own words and modified to fit a more modern magical practice. And while this book may prove valuable to researchers or historians, it is written more for practitioners who are looking not only for authentic lore and practice, but also for a creative guidebook that can help them pull from the past and inform the present in their own practice.

Although this book focuses primarily on the Celtic tradition, many other cultures play a part in its pages. It is important to remember that, even in ancient times, these cultures were connected by both vibrant commercial trade and rich cultural interactions. Thus many of the practices described here may have not originated with the Celts, but rather were brought to their land by other cultures and then practiced and handed down by their descendants. Did the Celts practice in the specific ways given here? We don't know for sure. But we do know that these practices are deeply entrenched in the culture and lore of the lush green islands that make up the traditionally Celtic lands. Modern practitioners can modify these practices and substitute elements and ingredients found in their own cultures and environments. There is nothing more delightful than working with water because of the variety of practices it offers. We can work with all bodies of water and in so many vastly different ways. From charm waters to sacred baths, from holy wells to the sea, from green plants to ancient fossils, water magic is full of so much power and mystery.

The fair folk are also important players in the tales told by this book. You can't, after all, immerse yourself in Celtic or Brythonic lore without acknowledging the role they play in many of the mythological and folk stories that are part of the heritage of the UK. In fact, the fair folk are still revered and honored as part of this culture today. The faery faith never really left the UK and, in the past few years, there has been a rebirth of interest in faery folklore around the world. It is almost as if the fair folk are calling out to be heard—challenging us to wake up and honor the land as we once did, to remember the old ways and use them to change our world for the better. If we don't use our witchcraft as a force for positive change, then what is it for?

I hope you have enjoyed the information and exercises provided in this book. I hope they inspire you in your own practice and draw you closer to water and the spirits that dwell within it. Remember: Water absorbs and amplifies energies and is a source of sacred transformation in and of itself. Use the old charms, create new recipes, and above all find purpose and pleasure in the sacred waters of the faery lands.

Conclusion

Bibliography

Allason-Jones, Lindsay and Bruce MacKay. *Coventina's Well: A Shrine on Hadrian's Wall*. Trustees of the Clayton Collection, Chesters Museum, 1985.

The Antiquary: A Magazine Devoted to the Study of the Past, Notes and Queries, vol. 22, 1890, pp. 103–105., doi:10.1093/nq/s6-i.2.48a.

Arrowsmith, Nancy, et al. *A Field Guide to the Little People*. London: Macmillan London Limited, 1977.

Beck, Horace and Marine Historical Association. *Folklore of the Sea*. Edison, NJ: Castle Books, 1999.

Black, George Fraser. *Scottish Charms and Amulets*. Printed by Neill and Co., 1894.

Boyer, Corinne. *Under the Witching Tree: A Folk Grimoire of Tree Lore and Practicum*. London: Troy Books, 2017.

———. "The Gathering Basket," *The Gathering Basket*, no. 17, June 2016.

Breen, Katlyn. *Ocean Amulets*. Self-published: Mermade, 1988.

Buckland, Raymond. *Scottish Witchcraft & Magick: The Craft of the Picts*. St. Paul, MN: Llewellyn, 2001.

Campbell, John Gregorson and Ronald Black. *The Gaelic Otherworld: John Gregorson Campbell's Superstitions of the Highlands & Islands of Scotland and Witchcraft & Second Sight in the Highlands & Islands*. Edinburgh: Birlinn, 2008.

Carmichael, Alexander. *Carmina Gadelica: Hymns and Incantations, with Illustrative Notes on Words, Rites, and Customs, Dying and Obsolete*. Edinburgh: Floris Books, 2006.

Clary, James. *Superstitions of the Sea*. St. Clair, MI: Maritime History in Art, 1994.

D'Arras, Jean. *Melusine; of the Noble History of Lusignan*. University Park, PA: The Pennsylvania State University Press, 2012.

Davies, Sioned. *The Mabinogion: A New Translation*. New York: Oxford World's Classics, 2008.

D'Este, Sorita and David Rankine. *Visions of the Cailleach: Exploring the Myths, Folklore and Legends of the Pre-Eminent Celtic Hag Goddess*. London: Avalonia, 2009.

Emoto, Masaru. *The Hidden Messages in Water*. Hillsboro, OR: Beyond Words Publishing, 2004.

Frazer, James George. *The Golden Bough*. New York: Macmillan, 1974.

Gary, Gemma. *Wisht Waters*. Richmond Vista, CA: Three Hands Press, 2013.

Howard, Michael. *Welsh Witches and Wizards*. Richmond Vista, CA: Three Hands Press, 2009.

Hunt, Robert. *Cornish Fairies*. Penryn, Cornwall: Tor Mark Press, 1995.

King, Graham. *British Book of Spells and Charms: A Compilation of Traditional Folk Magic*. London: Troy Books, 2016.

Kynes, Sandra. *Sea Magic: Connecting with the Ocean's Energy*. Woodbury, MN: Llewellyn Publications, 2008.

Lecouteux, Claude and Jon E. Graham. *A Lapidary of Sacred Stones: Their Magical and Medicinal Powers Based on the Earliest Sources*. Rochester, VT: Inner Tradition, 2012.

Leland, Charles Godfrey. *Gypsy Sorcery and Fortune Telling: Illustrated by Numerous Incantations, Specimens of Medical... Magic, Anecdotes and Tales (Classic Reprint)*. New York, New York: Castle Books, 1995.

Macgregor, Alexander. *Highland Superstitions: Connected with the Druids, Fairies, Witchcraft, Second-Sight, Hallowe'en, Sacred Wells and*

Bibliography

Lochs, with Several Curious Instances of Highland Customs and Beliefs. London: Gibbings & Company, Limited, 1901.

Mackinlay, James M. *Folklore of Scottish Lochs and Springs.* Glasgow:Reprinted by General Books LLC, 2011.

Mchardy, Stuart. *The Quest for the Nine Maidens.* Trowbridge: Luath Press Limited, 2003.

McNeill, F. Marian. *The Silver Bough.* Edinburgh: Stuart Titles, 1989.

Morgan, Adrian. *Toads & Toadstools.* Berkeley, CA: Celestial Arts, 1995.

Owen, Elias. *Welsh Folk-Lore: A Collection of the Folk-Tales and Legends of North Wales.* 1887. Reprinted Oxford: Filiquarian Publishing LLC, 1955.

Pearson, Nigel G. *Devil's Plantation: East Anglian Lore, Witchcraft & Folk-Magic.* London: Troy Books, 2016.

Quiller-Couch, Arthur. *Sacred Wells—A Study in the History, Meaning, and Mythology of Holy Wells & Water.* 2nd ed., New York: Algora Publishing, 2009.

Ross, Anne. *The Folklore of the Scottish Highlands.* New York: Tempus, 1993.

Sikes, Wirt. *British Goblins: Welsh Folklore, Fairy Mythology, Legends and Traditions.* Memphis, TN: General Books, 2010.

The Stratagems, and the Aqueducts of Rome, by Sextus Julius. Frontinus et al., Cambridge, MA: Harvard University Press, 1925.

Thomas, W. Jenkyn. *The Welsh Fairy Book.* London: Forgotten Books, 2007.

Varner, Gary R. *Water from the Sacred Well.* Raleigh, NC: Lulu Com, 2010.

Whelan, Edna. *The Magic and Mystery of Holy Wells.* Chieveley, Berks: Capall Bann, 2001.

Wilby, Emma. *Cunning Folk and Familiar Spirits Shamanistic Visionary Traditions in Early Modern British Witchcraft and Magic.* Brighton, UK: Sussex Academic Press, 2010.

Internet Resources

Museum of Witchcraft and Magic, *museumofwitchcraftandmagic*
  .co.uk/.

Smithsonian Institution, *www.smithsonianmag.com/*.

Welsh Texts, *www.maryjones.us/*.

Coulson, Laura. "Legends of the Shellycoat." *www.academia*
  .edu/34879481/Legends_of_the_Shellycoat.

Hurst, Brian. "Fountains." *www.gardening-uk.com/waterlands/*
  fountains/index.html.

"Magick in Theory and Practice—Introduction and Theorems."
  www.sacred-texts.com/oto/aba/defs.htm.

Miller, Jason. "Dion Fortune Is Attributed the Saying: 'Magic Is
  the Art of Changing Consciousness at Will." What Role Do
  You See the Ability to Change or Alter One's Own Consciousness as Playing in Magical Practice?" *strategicsorcery*
  .blogspot.com/2010/06/dion-fortune-is-attributed-saying-is.html.

"The Holy Wells of Somerset." *people.bath.ac.uk/liskmj/living-spring/*
  sourcearchive/fs2/fs2jb1.htm.

"The Roman Baths." *www.romanbaths.co.uk/*.

"Water." *whatthebleep.com/water-crystals*.

Index of Magical Exercises

Chapter 1: The Magic of Water

Creating a Water Altar   21

Water Glyph Meditation   31

Chapter 2: River Witches

Aligning with a River Spirit   43

Grounding Bath with Drain Release   51

The Waterfall   54

The Protective Bubble   55

The Ice Wall   56

The Tidal Wave   56

Sacred Water Blessing   62

Waning Moon Cleansing   63

Crystal Spray   63

Herbal Spray   64

A Quick Daily Herbal Asperge   64

Full Moon Purification Bath   65

Chapter 3: Sacred Well Witches

Clootie Charm   101

Entering the Faery Realm   102

Chapter 5: Marsh Witches
Dark Still Waters Meditation   151

Chapter 6: Sea Witches
Moon Gazing   161
Protect the Dolphins   189

Chapter 7: Local Water Spirits
Choosing an Offering   203
Raising and Contacting Spirits   204

Chapter 8: Mermaids and Finfolk
Enchanting a Mirror   232
Combing the Water   233
Dark Moon Mermaid Bath   235

Chapter 9: Water Witchery
Making Flower Water   241
Making Direct Gemstone Elixirs   242
Making Indirect Gemstone Elixirs   243

Index of Magical Exercises

To Our Readers

Weiser Books, an imprint of Red Wheel/Weiser, publishes books across the entire spectrum of occult, esoteric, speculative, and New Age subjects. Our mission is to publish quality books that will make a difference in people's lives without advocating any one particular path or field of study. We value the integrity, originality, and depth of knowledge of our authors.

Our readers are our most important resource, and we appreciate your input, suggestions, and ideas about what you would like to see published.

Visit our website at *www.redwheelweiser.com* to learn about our upcoming books and free downloads, and be sure to go to *www.redwheelweiser.com/newsletter* to sign up for newsletters and exclusive offers.

You can also contact us at *info@rwwbooks.com* or at

Red Wheel/Weiser, LLC
65 Parker Street, Suite 7
Newburyport, MA 01950

About the Author

Annwyn Avalon is a witch and priestess, and the founder of Triskele Rose, an Avalonian witchcraft tradition. Annwyn writes the Patheos Pagan blog, *The Water Witch*, and is an award-winning, internationally known dancer with a repertoire of water and mermaid themed belly dance performances.